West of Eden

**A Christian Perspective
of the New Age Movement**

David McDowell

Companion Press
P.O. Box 310
Shippensburg, PA 17257-0310

"Good Stewards of the
Manifold Grace of God"

ISBN 1-56043-537-2

For Worldwide Distribution
Printed in the U.S.A.

Contents

INTRODUCTION

The New Age Movement (N.A.M.) has been called the religion with a designer label. It is a cultural trend that has been "faddish" for several years, and there are few parts of this country that do not know of its existence.

The real impact of the N.A.M., however, will be made long after it has ceased being avant-garde. As long as it is a trend, its influence will be perceptible. Once it loses its novelty and is no longer hyped by movie stars and late night psychics, it will begin to do its most pervasive and deadly work. The reason? It will have entered the mainstream of Western thought and culture.

I have written this book as a member of a society whose Judeo-Christian foundations are being severely challenged by this New Age spirituality. I have also written as a pastor who desires his flock to have a clear biblical worldview and to avoid being drawn into the syncretism and ambiguity of the N.A.M.

This book has grown out of my study and preparation for numerous lectures and seminars given on campuses and in churches, in both the United States and Australia. I have been encouraged to formalize my thoughts so they can be more readily accessible to a broader audience.

I view this book as a general introduction to the N.A.M. Although it is by no means the definitive work on the subject, this volume does cover a wide range of topics and will provide the reader a wealth of information. It is entitled *West of Eden* because I believe that the basic belief system of the N.A.M. was expressed in the temptation by satan in Eden (Genesis 3:1-6). This system has now moved westward and is making a great impact on our culture.

In Chapter 1, I attempt to give a general overview of the N.A.M., including my own comprehensive definition. I use the word attempt, not out of humility so much as in recognition of the amorphous nature of the movement. Chapter 2 provides the reader with a picture of how the N.A.M. has influenced our culture. In Chapter 3, there is an historical overview of the N.A.M.'s development in America. Chapter 4 contains a theological critique that I believe may be my most important contribution. Here I set forth a "window grid" that compares the major doctrines of the Christian faith with the New Age worldview. The inspiration for this idea came from a presentation by John DeVries at a Third World seminar in India in 1985, which I attended.

In Chapter 5, I suggest areas of agreement that Christians can have with the N.A.M. They are followed by the crucial areas of disagreement in Chapter 6. Chapter 7 offers some practical suggestions on ways to communicate the gospel with those in the N.A.M. It is my firm belief that most New Agers are seeking a true understanding of God, and that they need to be treated with respect as well as with a recognition that they are being deceived by the "god of this age" (2 Corinthians 4:4).

I have included appendices on specific topics, in addition to questions for individual comprehension or group discussion following most chapters. There is also a glossary of terms and a bibliography of suggested reading and research material located at the end of the book.

It is my prayer that those who read this volume will be greatly helped to better understand the times in which they live and the God of Truth for whom they seek.

* * * * * *

My thanks to all those who helped proofread portions of this document, especially to my wife Gloria who was so gentle on my ego. Special thanks also go to Fran Fern who put all of my hen-scratchings on computer and then re-typed the entire thing after the computer ate the first copy; to Cathie McCoy who helped tremendously in the last-minute proofing and "cleaning up" of the manuscript; to Bill and Joan Johansen who gave me special encouragement to complete this manuscript; and to my faithful family and friends who provided prayer and financial support for this project.

I want to dedicate this book to the glory of God and to the members and friends of the College Church, Northampton, Massachusetts, in honor of its twentieth anniversary. It is a church that shares both the spiritual heritage of Jonathan Edwards and a desire to once again see the Holy Spirit's presence overshadow its town.

David P. McDowell
Northampton, MA
August 1992

My Dear Wormwood,

I wonder you should ask me whether it is essential to keep the patient ignorant of your own existence. That question, at least for the present phase of the struggle, has been answered for us by the High Command [satan]. Our policy, for the moment, is to conceal ourselves. Of course this has not always been so. We are really faced with a cruel dilemma. When the humans disbelieve in our existence we lose all the pleasing results of direct terrorism, and we make no magicians. On the other hand, when they believe in us, we cannot make them materialists and skeptics. At least, not yet. I have great hopes that we shall learn in due time how to emotionalize and mythologize their science to such an extent that what is, in effect, a belief in us (though not under that name) will creep in while the human mind remains closed to belief in the Enemy [God]. The "Life Force," the worship of sex, and some aspects of Psychoanalysis may here prove useful. If once we can produce our perfect work—the Materialist Magician, the man, not using, but veritably worshipping, what he calls "Forces" while denying the existence of "spirits"— then the end of the war will be in sight. But in the meantime we must obey our orders. I do not think you will have much difficulty in keeping the patient in the dark. The fact that "devils" are predominantly *comic* figures in the modern imagination will help you. If any faint suspicion of your existence begins to arise in his mind, suggest to him a picture of something in red tights, and persuade him that since he cannot believe in that (it is an old textbook method of confusing them) he therefore cannot believe in you.

Your affectionate uncle
Screwtape[*]

[*] C.S. Lewis, *The Screwtape Letters*. NY: Macmillan, 1961, 1968, pp. 32-33

Chapter 1

An Overview of the *New Age Movement* (N.A.M.)

"When the moon is in the Seventh House,
And Jupiter aligns with Mars.
Then Peace will guide the planets,
And Love will steer the stars.
This is the Dawning of the Age of Aquarius..."

If you are an early baby-boomer, you may remember dancing to this song from the 1968 musical "Hair." However, you may have had your mind on things other than the message of the words. This song was actually an astrological prediction that had its roots in the ancient Hopi, Aztec and Mayan civilizations. This prophecy refers to a time, toward the end of earth's history, when the planets would align themselves in a certain arrangement. This configuration would usher in and energize a new age of harmony and unity. The date? August 16 and 17, 1987, known as the days of the Interplanetary Harmonic Convergence.

Approximately 144,000 people worldwide gathered to celebrate this occasion. Some participants claimed that the "flow of energy" from the converging planets moved from person to person as they joined hands and deepened their own "self-realization" through meditation. They claimed they felt all strife and hostility move from the Earth into space as they together intoned the Hindu word *OM.** Many believed the ancient Mayan prophecy that there would now be only twenty-five years left for the liberation and harmony of the planet or else it would face destruction.[1] This means that, in the year 2012, our earth will see either annihilation or the dawning of a New Age.

I venture to guess that you might be raising your eyebrows at what you have read thus far. However, despite your skepticism, there is a growing number of people in our country and in our world who are "true believers" in a new religious consciousness. Many have defined this time in astrological terms as the end of *Pisces*, the age of

---

*   OM: pronounced Ah-Oh-Um, each syllable representing one of the three states of human consciousness; when pronounced together, he is said to enter the fourth state of consciousness, which is cosmic unity. In other words, while humming OM, one's self (Atman) becomes God (Brahman).

faith characterized by the Judeo-Christian religions, and the beginning of the age of *Aquarius*, a
new age of knowledge and religious experience.

Norman Paulsen, founder of the Sunburst Com-
munities, in an interview with *New Age Dawn*
magazine, describes the Age of Aquarius as an age
where the religious seeker is no longer satisfied
with traditional Christianity: "I had to get my
hands on God, and see him and know him. I could
never be satisfied just to take somebody's word for
it...the old age of Pisces says, 'Let's have
faith'...the new Aquarian age says, 'I know.' "[2]

America has always been a breeding ground for
unique religious movements. In the period between 1820 and 1860, there emerged a host of new
religious groups during a time of great social
change: Shakers, Mormons, Campbellites, Mil-
lerites, and others. When we look at the recent
past, there is evidence that our quest for newness
in religious experience has taken us into uncharted
waters. Eldon G. Ernst, a religious historian,
writes, "The range of the 'new' in contemporary
religious life and thought has moved beyond the
experience of earlier generations. The movement is
away from the boundaries of the Judeo-Christian
heritage of Western civilization."[3]

This quest for newness has opened the soul of
America to the growing influence of Asian
spirituality. Eastern religious thought has been in
this country for a long time, but now its influence
is far more pervasive and normalized. Ron Enroth

declares, "Thirty years ago in the United States one might have thought that a *guru* was an exotic animal. Today, because of Zen and other Eastern spiritual disciplines, it is practically a household word."[4]

Perspectives of the New Age Movement

The goal of this first chapter is to answer the question, "What is the New Age Movement?" A concise definition will eventually be given, but first we will examine the N.A.M. from various perspectives. These will serve to demonstrate not only the incredible scope of the movement, but also its indescribable character.

Constantly Changing

Our first perspective comes from *Time* magazine (Dec. 7, 1987), which defined the New Age Movement as "...a shifting kaleidoscope of beliefs, fads, and rituals." A casual glance at a mailing from Pyramid Books of Salem, Massachusetts, will confirm this statement. Pyramid carries over 8,000 titles on dozens of New Age subjects, including: astrology, Eastern philosophy, psychic and spiritual development, health, nutrition, aromatherapy, meditation, reincarnation, auras, chakras, channeling, crystals, gems, Native American spirituality and women's studies. It also touts such items as: herbs for magic and healing, angel cards, tarot decks, talismans, goddess figures, rune and ethnic jewelry, crystal balls, pyramids, gem therapy charts, natal charts, love scopes, Boji stones, chants and devotional tapes, Tibetan bells and gongs, subliminal tapes and New Age music tapes. (If some of these terms are unfamiliar, you may want to make use of the glossary at the end of the book.)

Widespread and Growing

Another perspective shared by many critics of the N.A.M., such as Constance Cumbey, Dave Hunt and Tex Mares, is that it is a well-organized conspiracy just waiting to take over the world. I personally do not hold to the conspiracy theory. I do believe, however, that it is a growing confederacy of groups and movements from nearly every sector of life: the health field, politics, science, psychology, sports, the military, religion, ecology, education, music, art, etc.

There is no umbrella organization to join or universal creed to confess, but New Age adherents in all those areas of life are bound together by a shared worldview and a common vision. They envision the transformation of the world through a new spirituality that will cause the rethinking of traditional political and economic structures and will bring about equality and world peace. These groups also share information and ideas through a system of networking in New Age journals and magazines. Thus, it is more clarifying to think of the N.A.M. as a change in the way our culture views the world, rather than as a global conspiracy.

Marilyn Ferguson, one of the prime movers of the movement, describes the N.A.M. as:

a leaderless but powerful network...working to
bring about radical change in the United States.
Its members have broken with certain key elements of Western thought, and they may even
have broken continuity with history. This network is the Aquarian Conspiracy. [She defines
conspire literally as "to breath together."] It is a
conspiracy without a political doctrine. Without a
manifesto...this benign conspiracy for a new
human agenda has triggered the most rapid cultural alignment in history. The great shuddering,
irrevocable shift overtaking us is not a new political, religious, or philosophical system. It is a new
mind—the ascendance of a startling worldview
that gathers into its framework breakthrough
science and insights from earliest recorded
thought.[5]

Although we cannot deny the growing influence
of New Age thought on our culture, neither should
we jump to the conclusion that it is a well-planned
conspiracy. The prophet Isaiah was warned by God
"not to say, 'It is a conspiracy!' in regard to all that
this people call a conspiracy, and you are not to
fear what they fear or be in dread of it" (Isaiah
8:12). The reason is, the conspiracies of this world
mean nothing to a sovereign God. He alone should
be feared because He is holy and His infinite
power is too great for the forces of evil (see Psalm
2:1-6). The Christian should not be immobilized
by talk of conspiracy, nor should he give up hope
of reaching his own culture because of the growth
of the N.A.M.[6]

Basic Components

A third perspective can be gained by recognizing the spiritual components of the N.A.M. You will find some combination of the following in all groups and organizations that are a part of the New Age.

1. **Mysticism.** The belief that God (Ultimate Reality) is known by experience and not through the rational mind. This knowledge of God cannot be expressed in words or doctrine; it can only be understood intuitively. Therefore, truth is not something we should investigate with our minds, but rather experience with our hearts.

2. **Syncretism.** A belief that all religions teach the same thing. Though the externals of these religions seem to differ, they are in essence the same. There may be many paths to the one truth, but these differences are superficial. Thus the uniqueness of Christianity must be denied and Jesus of Nazareth considered merely one manifestation of cosmic consciousness.

3. **Monism.** A belief that everything which exists is a part of one (mono) continuous reality. It means that there are no ultimate differences between a man, a woman, a squirrel, a radish, a rock, a blueberry muffin and God. "All is One" and any perceived differences between things that we see are imaginary.

4. **Pantheism.** In its simplest form, a belief that God and the universe are identical. The divine is not identified with a personal being, but is rather a universal presence, consciousness or force diffused throughout all things. This "All is God" belief lays the groundwork for "I am God." (**Panentheism**, a variation of the former, believes that although everything is a part of God, not everything is God. The divine is separated from the cosmos but lives His life in and through it.)

5. **Narcissism.** A term that connotes an unhealthy self-centeredness. (Named after the legendary Narcissus, a handsome Greek youth condemned by the gods to desire his own image.) New Age proponents believe that the self is deified and is the very center of the universe. This self-as-God is believed to have the power to create and to control reality.

6. **Occultism.** A belief in hidden or secret wisdom that must be learned so the self will experience and control the powers of the universe. This wisdom can be gained through such occult practices as astrology, palm reading, crystal gazing, channeling and other forms of divination.

Old Ideas with a New Face

An earlier issue of *Time* magazine (1979) provides us with a fourth perspective on the N.A.M. "...the New Age is a combination of spirituality and superstition, fad and farce, about which the only thing certain is that it is *not new*."[7]

This definition is reinforced by a cartoon in *New Yorker* magazine that depicts the directors of a cereal company seated in the boardroom. On the table in front of them is a box of breakfast cereal with the word "New" on it. The chairman asks, "So what's so new about it?" The response is, "Sir, the word *New* on the box is what's new."

As *Time* has stated, there's nothing really new in the N.A.M. It is, in reality, a resurgence of some very old traditions such as:

Paganism (e.g. witchcraft, both ancient and feminist);
Occultism (spiritualism, channeling, psychic phenomena);
Native American religion (Shamanism);
Eastern religions (Hinduism, Buddhism, Taoism, Zoroastrianism);
Gnosticism (ancient second century heresy).

These ancient traditions, so foreign to our Western mind-set, have been attractively packaged in a box marked "New" to appeal to our spiritually starved culture, which has lost its appetite for the Judeo-Christian heritage.

Humanity Is Divine

A fifth perspective on the N.A.M. is revealed when one considers its primary goal: the transformation of consciousness; a complete change in the way people view reality. It teaches that "All is One, All is God; therefore, We are God." Essentially this means a belief that humanity is divinity and that the main problem of our existence is not sin, but the ignorance of our divine status. The way we "raise our consciousness" to our true identity is by the use of "spiritual technology," which includes: yoga, meditation, hypnosis, bodily disciplines, martial arts, mysticism and human potential seminars. When enough individuals transform their consciousness, it will effect global change. Therefore, the bumper sticker "Think Peace" communicates more than a slogan. It reveals the belief that if enough people exercise the unlimited potential of their divinity by visualizing a peaceful planet, then they will bring such a reality into existence.[8]

Man Is the Measure of All Things

A sixth perspective is the identification of the N.A.M. as Cosmic Humanism.[9] Secular Humanism jettisoned God and placed man as supreme in the universe. It also determined reality by what we perceive with our five senses. This materialistic perspective has proven itself inadequate to meet the needs of modern man. It has systematically denied the existence of the divine and, therefore, failed to satisfy the innate spiritual hunger in each of us. In reaction, a cosmic form of humanism has evolved that still sees man at the center of the universe. God, however, has been reintroduced into the system and is none other than man himself!

One would question whether this new humanism really offers a progressive form of spirituality to our desperate world. Is it not a step backward into the old age of "magick" and superstition?

> The essence of the magical worldview is a belief in a homocentric [man-centered] universe. Man is literally the microcosm [the little world of human nature] reflecting the macrocosm [the universe], so that the macrocosm in turn is a projection of man. Hence all things—stars, herbs, stones, metals, planets, the elements, the elemental—mesh with man, his longings, his lusts, his desires, his fears, and even his physical appearance and health. Each natural object and natural phenomenon has a direct influence upon some aspect of man's body or psyche, and man's actions can in turn affect the elements. All things are made for man and on the model of man. Magic is a doctrine that, far more than religion or science, exalts man to the loftiest regions of glory: hence its perennial attraction...[10]

Humanity in Control

The final perspective on the N.A.M. is revealed in its emphasis upon power and control. The Bible makes it clear that the essence of true religion is submission to and trust in the God who has revealed Himself in Jesus Christ. The essence of magic is self-glorification and control. "True religion, specifically Christianity, prostrates itself before the throne of God, acknowledges man's inadequacy and helplessness before

Him, and implores His gracious help. Magic, on the other hand, seeks to control the forces of the universe, be they natural or supernatural."[11]

There is little wonder, then, that the N.A.M. has become so popular in a culture that is out of control because of the breakdown of the family, the disappearance of moral "markers" and the loss of a transcendent God. Instead of man being subjected to a pawn-like destiny before the "forces" of the universe, the N.A.M. offers a way by which humanity can reach out through occult knowledge and ritual technique to understand, grasp and ultimately control the universe.[12]

Summary Definition of the New Age Movement

The N.A.M. is really nothing new. It is a hybrid mix of paganism, occultism, Eastern religions and ancient Gnosticism, attractively packaged for a spiritually starved Western culture. To a world living under the threat of extinction, it promises unity, power, peace and prosperity on a global scale. Such hope is found in changing the way we see the world through a transformation of consciousness, which includes the realization that we ourselves are gods and that we must unleash our divine potential for the good of the world.

Are you still feeling a bit confused about the N.A.M.? You may feel that what has been said so far has merely helped to tighten your grip on a wet bar of soap. Please keep on reading. You may find that interacting with the following questions increases your comprehension of the material you have just read. Also, in our next chapter, you will be introduced to some specific examples of New Age influences on our culture.

Questions for Individual Comprehension or Group Discussion

1. What is the Age of Aquarius? What significance do many people find in its following the Age of Pisces?

2. What makes the N.A.M. different from other religious movements that have dotted the American scene?

3. How would you articulate the primary goal of the N.A.M.?

4. What do you think there is about human nature that makes us so prone to follow after the "new"?

5. Try to develop a concise definition of the N.A.M. that you can remember and use when evaluating certain groups and practices. Write it down.

6. Read Romans 1:21-25. What parts of this passage apply to what you know thus far about the N.A.M.?

Chapter 2

New Forms for an Old Lie

The N.A.M. has repackaged some very ancient traditions in order to appeal to our spiritually destitute Western culture. This Movement is so subtle and pervasive that many are exposing themselves to its influence without even being aware of it. New Age thought has a strong appeal to the "felt-needs" of modern day people in their search for meaning, value and significance.

Music

New Age music is growing at an overwhelming rate. Such instruments as the flute, guitar, harp, cello and synthesizer are blended into relaxing harmonies with background sounds like waves or rippling brooks (sounds made from a sheet of steel balanced on a balloon in water). It is music to meditate by, as seen from the titles: "Music for an

Inner Journey" or "Through the Portals of In-
finity." There is nothing inherently wrong with
New Age music as an art form. In fact, it is very en-
joyable and relaxing. It becomes an issue, however,
when the music is used to induce a "contentless"
meditative state or a mystical experience. These
practices are based upon a worldview incompatible
with the Christian faith.

Teaching Tools

Subliminal tapes are being marketed by *Syber-
vision, Mind Communications* and *Potentials Unlimited*. These tapes are designed to unlock the
"golden treasure of your subconscious powerhouse"
and "awaken your own hidden talents." The presupposition here is, when your subconscious mind
is brought into harmony with your conscious
thoughts and desires, you can do anything. These
audio tapes contain vocal messages hidden
beneath the level of consciousness and behind the
background sounds of soothing music or ocean
surf. There are tapes on the following:

No-Effort Weight Loss

Smoking

Tennis

Decision Making

Bed Wetting

Agoraphobia (a fear of open places)

Broken Relationships

Sex Life

Money/Prosperity

Developing Your Psychic Abilities

Astral Projection (out-of-body travel)

For example, a tape on *How to Quit Smoking* contains such subliminal messages as: "smoking makes me nauseous," "my breath smells," "I don't need nicotine," "I have the power to quit," "I am in control of my world," etc. One can see the emphasis on the power and control alleged to be locked away in our subconscious just waiting to be unleashed on any problem we face.

Does such a reliance upon personal power square with the reality of our lives? Have we really experienced lasting freedom from habits and behaviors that enslave us? Is not our condition more accurately described by St. Paul in Romans 7:15-24? He writes, "For that which I am doing, I do not understand; for I am not practicing what I would like to do, but I am doing the very thing I hate...For the good that I wish, I do not do; but I practice the very evil that I do not wish... Wretched man that I am! Who will set me free from the body of this death?" Paul's answer was found not in releasing his hidden potential, but in trusting what God did for him through the death and resurrection of Jesus Christ. This answer is a powerful antidote to smoking or any other life-dominating issue.

Athletics/Military

Sports Mind, Inc. is based in Seattle and works primarily in the area of athletic training. One of its clients has been the U.S. Army. In 1982 the company formulated an eight-week, $50,000 training program at Fort Hood, Texas, in which traditional calisthenics were replaced by holistic stretching and exercise techniques such as yoga, deep breathing and centering (focusing the mind so as to block out all thoughts and distractions). Apparently the training proved so successful that the Army expanded Sports Mind's assignment into a year-long, $350,000 program to help train Green Berets. These soldiers were taught meditation techniques so they could spend long hours hidden in enemy territory without the need for food or movement.[1]

National Defense

The Department of Defense has funded research projects on meditation, biofeedback and psychic phenomena.[2] (Remember to use the glossary for the definitions of these terms.) One example is the First Earth Battalion, also called the Natural Guard (Delta Force). "It is projected to be a New Age militia of warrior-monks, spiritually attuned to new methods of conflict resolution through yoga, meditation and the martial arts...its key innovator, Jim Channon, was funded by the U.S. Army to produce a multimedia presentation on the battalion, which was shown to the senior class at West Point."[3] Delta Force is no longer under study, but it did introduce New Age ideas into the military. In addition, the Army War College did a study in the early 1980's aimed at creating a New Age Army.[4] The study was never completed.

Education

"Confluent education," developed by Beverly Galyean, is making inroads into the public schools, especially in California. It includes the use of yoga, biofeedback and guided imagery to introduce children to the Inner-Self, the self that can guide them and help them make decisions. Parents should be aware that New Age thought enters the curriculum usually through a "piggyback" approach. In other words, it attaches itself to programs that have such laudable intentions as encouraging self-esteem, improving memory, reducing stress or cultivating creativity. This is not to say that all such programs are New Age. If in doubt, however, here are some questions for a concerned parent to ask:

1. Does the program espouse a particular religious worldview?

2. What is the educational value of such a program?

3. Does it have any relevance to the subject taught?

4. Is the program outside the teacher's credentialed field?

If you detect New Age spirituality, then you may request a program exemption for your child and/or a program's withdrawal from the curriculum if you are able to prove its presence.

You should also be aware that the courts recognize many movements other than Christianity and traditional orthodoxy as "religion." For example, in *Thomas* v. *Review Board*, 450 U.S. 707 (1981), the Supreme Court established that a viewpoint can constitute a religion if it is based upon religious training and belief, even if it is not a part of a church's official creed. Also, in *Torcaso* v. *Watkins*, 367 U.S. 488 (1961), the court even recognized Secular Humanism as a religion: "Among religions in this country which do not teach what would be generally considered a belief in the existence of God are Buddhism, Taoism, Ethical Culture, Secular Humanism, and others...." New Age beliefs would certainly fall under this definition because of its close connection with Eastern religious thought.[5]

New Age Bookstores

The New Age industry has exploded with growth in the past few years. In 1988 there were 25,000 titles in print, accounting for more than a billion dollars in sales. Waldenbooks said that sales of New Age titles jumped from 25 to 900 a week, after Shirley MacLaine's miniseries *Out on a Limb* was produced. Also, as of 1988, there were some 2500 bookstores that specialized in New Age books; double the number in 1982.[6]

A trip through a New Age bookstore may be an intimidating experience for many Christians. Some may have a conviction against exposing themselves to anything in the occult. Others have a fear of the unknown, based upon hearsay or an overactive imagination. Therefore, let me describe some of the items which have such a growing appeal to the curious as well as to the seeker of truth:

1. Jewelry. You will find some very symbolic and expensive jewelry, demonstrating how the New Age perspective has mainstreamed the ancient talisman (fetish) into the very world of fashion. For example, you could purchase card one of the Tarot deck in a 14K gold pendant. The picture is of "The Magician," who is alleged to be a transmitter of cosmic power. It is suggested that you could experience this power for only $75 as you wear it around your neck. Another item is a sterling silver chime pendant that goes for $30. Tiny little chimes inside this spherical pendant produce a "celestial" tinkling sound every time you move. This piece of jewelry is designed to replicate the sound of bells that accompany meditation and other ceremonial practices of most Eastern religions.

2. Tarot Card Decks. The Tarot is a tool used within the occult for divination or fortune-telling. The symbolism of each card (e.g. the Magician, the Empress, the Fool, the Lovers) is believed to contain the secrets of the universe and is the key to the wisdom of the ages. Each card and the order in which it is drawn is supposed to reveal one's future or to give guidance for an important decision. There are nearly 2,000 variations of the

Tarot. For example, there is the Mythic Tarot based upon Greek mythological characters. There is the Arthurian Tarot which uses symbols of the Sword, the Grail, the Stone, etc. to divine the future and to deepen one's self-knowledge.

One will find other tools very much like the Tarot with which people claim to discern the future. Runes, for example, are an ancient Celtic method of divination. They are flat, stone-like pieces of ceramic, each etched with an alphabetic script that resembles hen-scratchings. There are twenty-five runes in a set and each is said to contain "instant" answers, while three or four in a certain arrangement are supposed to reveal innermost truths. Other tools are Personal Power Cards, which are to help one gain power over personal circumstances; Dream Cards, which put one in contact with the subconscious mind; Medicine Cards, which can help one learn the healing powers of animals; and Phoenix Cards, a method designed to help discover times and places of previous lifetimes.

3. Crystals. One will also find an assortment of quartz crystals, the prices of which range from a few dollars to a few hundred dollars. The pet rock days of the 1970's have been updated. Crystals are now a $100 million-per-year business. Scientifically speaking, quartz

crystals are used in industry as energy con-
ductors. They contain electrical resonance
and produce their own electricity when under
pressure. The New Age belief is that crystals
hold and amplify energy from the body and
align it with the energy flow of the universe.
There is also a belief that crystals direct the
healing qualities of cosmic energy to an
ailing part of the human body.

4. Astrology. Most New Age bookstores will
have an incredible array of information relating to the very ancient occult practice of
astrology. This pseudoscience seeks to de-
cipher the influence of the planets upon the
earth at the exact time an individual was
born. Through the charting of such influence,
an interpretation is made that supposedly
will give a detailed analysis of one's past,
present and future. Some bookstores are now
offering a computerized astrology report that
will help analyze any relationship as well as
reveal one's romantic and sexual potential.

The Media and Board Games

The movie industry and the companies that create popular games and toys have brought aspects
of the N.A.M. into our homes and into the minds of
our children. The following are examples of how occult and Eastern religious philosophy have been
popularized and marketed for our culture.

Star Wars: A movie trilogy created by George Lucas who openly believes that God is defined as "The Force." According to his biographer, Dale Polloch, "Lucas wanted to instill in children a belief in a supreme being—not a religious god, but a universal deity that he named The Force, a cosmic energy source that incorporates and consumes all living things."[7]

Dark Crystal: A fairy tale movie produced by the late Jim Henson, creator of the Muppets, in which evil (the Skecsees) does not overcome the good (the Mystics), but rather both are shown to be one and the same. This is classic Eastern religious and occult thought, where all distinctions are erased and everything becomes unified into the One.

The Smurfs: A popular cartoon on NBC since 1981. The cute little Smurfs spend all their days avoiding the evil plots of the wizard Gargamel. Papa Smurf is a Shaman and tries to protect his family from Gargamel. Magic, spells, incantations, amulets (magic charms), shrines and pentagrams are a regular part of this adventure.

A.L.F. (alien life form), *E.T.* and *Close Encounters*: These seek to normalize the presence of life from outer space which, in most cases, represent an endearing form of higher intelligence as well as psychic ability. The New Age infatuation with extraterrestrial life (and UFOs) follows a belief in the evolutionary nature of the universe and the basic "oneness" (monism) of all things.

Dungeons and Dragons: A Fantasy Role Playing (FRP) game with occult symbolism. It is a board game based upon Tolkien's *Lord of the Rings* trilogy, where each player selects a character whose role he will play. Players must memorize spells, incantations and rituals taken directly from black magic, witchcraft, voodoo and satanism.[8] Many have argued that the game poses no danger because it is merely fantasy. But others cite the danger of overidentification with the characters and the history of violence connected with the game.[9] The Christian must recognize that the game promotes the learning of things that are soundly condemned in the Scriptures. "There shall not be found among you anyone who makes his son or his daughter pass through the fire, one who uses divination, one who practices witchcraft, or one who interprets omens, or a scorcerer, or one who casts a spell, or a medium, or a spiritist, or one who calls up the dead" (Deuteronomy 18:10,11). It is hard to justify the position that God accepts in our imaginations what He would condemn in our behavior. Did not Jesus teach that the content of our hearts can be sinful though our behavior remains lawful?

Ouija Board: This number-one selling board game is, in reality, a tool designed to contact spirits and develop psychic abilities. It is based upon an ancient device dating back to the Chinese in the sixth century B.C. In 1853 a French spiritualist named Planchette created the board, similar to the present game board, and a heart-shaped, three-legged platform called the "planchette."[10] Therefore, what is to most merely a party game has its origins in the occult. The recreational use of the

Ouija is considered dangerous even by those who use it for its spiritualistic purposes. Stoker Hunt in his book, *Ouija: The Most Dangerous Game,* explores the history and legacy of the Ouija and presents a strong case against experimentation. (It should be noted that Hunt, a New Age believer, finishes his book by giving detailed instructions for using the Ouija if one is ready for it.)

Tell a Fortune: A new board game that uses the basics of astrology and a deck of fifty-four prediction cards to provide answers to specific questions. Each card holds a message and the board tells what area of one's life is affected. Once again we see human nature's fascination with the future. We also see how practices that once took place in darkened rooms and carnival sideshows have been mainstreamed into our living rooms.

Management Training and Business

Innovation Association of Framingham, Massachusetts, charges $1,650 for a three-day executive leadership development seminar designed to help organizations become "metanoic" (possessing a clear vision of one's goals and purpose).[11] Energy Unlimited of Crystal Lake, Illinois, charges $250 for a two-day course teaching people to walk over burning coals. The "logic" is that if a person can train his mind to endure fire walking, he has the unlimited potential to do anything.[12]

Social scientist Michael Ray invokes Zen, yoga and Tarot cards when he teaches his course on

"Creativity in Business" at the Stanford Graduate School of Business (*Time*, December 7, 1987).

Mason Sexton, graduate of Harvard Business School, now works on Wall Street and bases his predictions of the stock market on a combination of mathematics and astrology (*Time*, December 7, 1987).

In the July 24, 1987, issue of *The Wall Street Journal*, Peter Waldman writes, "Abuzz with buzzwords, corporate America has launched one of the most concerted efforts ever to change the attitudes and values of workers. Dozens of major U.S. companies—including Ford Motor Co., Proctor and Gamble Co., TRW Inc., Polaroid Corp., and Pacific Telesis Groups Inc.—are spending millions of dollars on so-called New Age workshops." Some of the more famous groups putting on these seminars are *Lifespring, Krone Seminars, MSIA, Pecos River Learning Center* and the *Trans Tech, Inc.*

The latter (T.T.I.) is a management consulting company, owned by Warner Erhard, that markets its New Age philosophy of human potential through a series of franchisers. A corporate client of one of these franchisers could buy Erhard's ideas and be totally unaware they had anything to do with the N.A.M.[13] The amazing thing is that most companies are willing to spend millions on such training with virtually no scrutiny of the product or the credentials of those who teach.

Research has been done on the effectiveness of many New Age techniques that claim to improve human performance and enhance personal development. A major study was done by the U.S. Army and the National Research Council (NRC). The results can be found in a 300-page paperback entitled, *Enhancing Human Performance: Issues, Theories and Techniques* (The National Academy Press, 1988). The study included various New Age psychotechnologies that are being used increasingly in the classrooms, boardrooms and locker rooms of our country and which tout incredible results. Techniques such as imaging for memory development, progressive relaxation therapy, biofeedback, alpha brain-wave states, mind-over-matter programs, left brain/right brain function, Neuro-Linguistic Programming and paranormal phenomena were among those discussed.

The outcome of this massive study revealed a lack of scientific evidence for the claims of these New Age technologies. The study also counseled organizations to carefully assess prospective programs on the basis of scientific evidence rather than on word-of-mouth recommendation. The reason is due to what the NRC calls "illusory covariation," a syndrome where program advocates will insist on a program's effectiveness even when such cannot be substantiated by scientific evidence or by a proven increase in performance level.

The Medical Profession

Nursing has come a long way since Florence Nightingale. Many of the mainline nursing textbooks reflect a New Age worldview. One of the more blatant New Age nursing texts is *Holistic Nursing* (1981), written by Barbara Blattner. Her book includes relaxation exercises in a chapter called "Psychic Healing Made Simple."[14] She also includes hatha yoga exercises (the goal of which is union with the "one"), complete from the opening chants to the closing mantra (a Hindu incantation).[15]

Other significant texts are *Holistic Nursing: A Handbook for Practice* (Dossey et al., 1988) and *Cardiovascular Nursing: Bodymind Tapestry* (1984). The latter is endorsed by the American Association of Critical Care Nurses and is the application of New Age principles to the intensive care unit. Both of these texts teach the importance of seeking wisdom from one's "inner advisor" through relaxation techniques. Respectability for this New Age nursing theory does not come through its emphasis on the occult, but in its appeal to science.[16] In other words, an Eastern religious worldview is hidden beneath scientific jargon so it will become believable to the Western mind.

New Age spirituality also can be seen in what is commonly called the Holistic Health Movement. Two of its most famous practitioners are Dr. O. Carl Simonton, Director of the Simonton Cancer Center in California, and Dr. Bernie Siegel, professor at Yale Medical School. Both use the therapeutic tool of *Visualization* as a medical treatment. They believe that, through visualization, a patient's immune system can be recreated to fight disease. The principle here is, each person has the power to create his own reality and must take responsibility for his own condition.

There are elements of valuable advice found in their work, such as the patient becoming responsible for his own health and the importance of compassion and hope on the part of the physician. However, their emphasis on creating reality through visualization and guided imagery is derived from Shamanism and is occult in origin.[17] We should not be deceived when such therapeutic tools come to us couched in pseudo-scientific language. The Bible's warning is clear: "See to it that no one takes you captive through philosophy and empty deception, according to the tradition of men, according to the elementary principles of the world, rather than according to Christ" (Colossians 2:8). (For a further discussion of visualization, see Appendix to Chapter 6.)

Chiropractic is another health profession in which New Age techniques have made inroads. Two major types of chiropractic are practiced by the estimated 39,000 chiropractors in the U.S. The largest group consists of about 32,000 "broad scope" chiropractors who use manipulation of the spine to restore nerve flow and function. They might also use other methods such as physical therapy and nutrition.

The other 7,000 chiropractors are known as "straight." These therapists believe that the body's life force ("Chi" or "qi") does all the healing. Therefore, "...they do not diagnose or treat specific conditions. Instead, they treat subluxations, or partial dislocations of the spine, in an effort to restore normal nerve flow...When you restore normal nerve flow and function...you can achieve optimal health and the body will express 100 percent of its life force."[18] Among this last group of chiropractors are those who practice the "Network" method. They believe in the life force approach, but in addition, they claim that the thin sheath covering the spinal cord holds imprints caused by physical, emotional or chemical stress. Thus, patients are encouraged to re-experience these traumatic events as adjustments are made on the spinal column. Such a release of tension and emotion allows the free flow of energy through the body, "which will naturally bring healing."

Acupuncture, in most cases, is another New Age therapeutic technique that is based upon the life force concept. The practitioner will insert long and very fine needles into specific spots of the body. It is believed that this stimulates or sedates the body's energy flow and brings it into proper balance. Acupressure is based upon the same principle, except fingertip pressure is used instead of a needle.

The theory behind most of these techniques (including "therapeutic touch") is that people are one with the universe, giving energy to it and receiving energy from it in a proper rhythm.[19] It is believed that this energy flows to the organs of the body through different pathways (twelve major meridians). New Age therapists believe that disease occurs when this rhythm is disturbed and the energy of the body becomes unbalanced. Health, or balance, can be reestablished when this energy or spiritual force is properly manipulated.

The life force concept, which forms the basis of "straight" chiropractic as well as acupuncture, cannot be substantiated by any scientific evidence. It is a belief system based upon an Eastern religious worldview. For this reason, I believe that these therapies are incompatible with Christianity and should not be used lest one expose himself to the "forces" of deception and the possibility of the demonic. Unfortunately, many Christians are seeking such therapies out of painful desperation. They want relief no matter what it costs or what its origin. Perhaps the Church needs some serious biblical instruction concerning the role of suffering in the Christian life. Could it be that the unwillingness to suffer physically is directly related to a weakness of the soul?

Ecology

The evolution revolution of Darwin "unseated" the God of the Bible as the creative force in the universe. Science, with its evolutionary hypothesis, had no room for the miraculous or mystical. Times have changed, however, and our culture has experienced the limits of science's ability to answer the deeper questions of the human spirit. Increasingly, science is willing to acknowledge the supernatural. A mechanistic, closed universe of Secular Humanism is being disputed and there is room once again for the mystical.

It is not the God of the Bible, however, that is now being enthroned, but a pagan deity: i.e. Gaia, the goddess of Nature or Mother Earth.[20] She is seen as the one from whom we have our origin and for whom we are responsible. (Note the religious fervor by some on Earth Day.) The earth is not just a ball of matter floating in space, "but a living planet, a living being, a consciousness."[21]

Read what Dr. James Lovelock, a British scientist working with NASA, said about Gaia:

> She is Mother Earth. Gaia is immortal. She is the eternal source of life. She is surely virgin. She does not need to reproduce herself as she is immortal. She is certainly the mother of us all, including Jesus...Gaia is not a tolerant mother. She is rigid and inflexible, ruthless in the destruction of whoever transgresses. Her unconscious objective is that of maintaining a world adapted to life. If we men hinder this objective we will be eliminated without pity.[22]

Perhaps we ought to design a new bumper sticker that says, "Love Your Mother or Else!" (You may want to refer to the glossary for definitions of two branches of New Age ecology: *Deep Ecology* and *Eco-Feminism.*)

Social Services

The hospice movement, which provides specialized care for the terminally ill, has its roots in the Christian faith and has always been open to the spiritual needs of the dying. However, because of its openness to "spiritual care," it is attracting many New Age advocates. Some local hospice groups are using textbooks in their volunteer training programs which are blatantly New Age.[23]

Many licensed counselors use various forms of Visualization and Guided Imagery combined with hypnosis as a therapy procedure.[24] Almost all of them cite a relationship to Carl Jung's psychotherapeutic technique. This topic will be discussed further in our next chapter.

Psychic Phenomena

We are seeing a renewed interest in and investigation of ESP in its various forms, such as telekinesis, clairvoyance, precognition and post-cognition. Just tune in to late night TV and see the proliferation of psychics and their Hollywood hosts. In a recent study done by the University of Chicago's National Opinion Research Council, two million Americans claim that they have had an out-of-body or near-death experience. Also, forty-two percent of American adults believe that they have been in contact with the dead. At least two-thirds of these same adults report having experienced ESP.[25]

Most people researching these phenomena believe that those who manifest psychic abilities are merely demonstrating natural abilities that are latent within them. Such abilities come through tapping a mysterious "energy field" or "force" of some kind. There is a denial among many in the N.A.M. that such paranormal manifestations have anything to do with the occult.

Contradicting this view, however, is the fact that many have acquired psychic abilities through personal experimentation with the occult, or through the laying on of hands by a psychic. Jean Dixon claimed to have received her "gift" when as a child an old gypsy took her hand and transferred power to her.[26]

Channeling is another trendy phenomenon as well as a lucrative business. Perhaps the term "medium" is more familiar to most people. A channeler (medium) is a person who goes into a trance-like state in order to establish contact with a spirit or "higher" consciousness. Jack Pursel is a well-known channeler for a spirit entity called Lazaris. At one time Pursel had a two-year waiting list for consultations at $93 an hour![27] Much of channeling can be explained by nothing more than great acting.[28] But the danger of channeling is the very real possibility that the channeled entity is an evil spirit who impersonates someone or something and whose goal it is to lead the inquirer away from the true God. That is accomplished by giving out a small amount of accurate information in order to gain credibility, followed by large doses of lies designed to mislead one into emotional dependence on its advice.[29]

Jesus issued this warning to those who were following satan's lies: "...He [satan] was a murderer from the beginning, and does not stand in the truth, because there is no truth in him. Whenever he speaks a lie, he speaks from his own nature; for he is a liar, and the father of lies" (John 8:44).

All forms of psychic practices are condemned in the Bible because they are seen as pathways leading away from God. Calling them "parapsychology" does not make them less dangerous to us or more acceptable to God. He has clearly communicated His thoughts on these things: "Do not turn to mediums or spiritists; do not seek them out to be defiled by them. I am the Lord your God" (Leviticus 19:31). "As for the person who turns to mediums and to spiritists, to play the harlot after them, I will set My face against that person and will cut him off from among his people" (Leviticus 20:6). There is no indication in the New Testament that He has changed His mind. In fact, it is recorded that St. Paul dealt harshly with a psychic who was hindering his preaching of the gospel. Acts 16:16-21 records that Paul discerned that this psychic was demonized and proceeded to exorcize the evil spirits from her.

Conclusion

All that we have seen in this chapter illustrates the pervasive effect the N.A.M. is having on our Western culture. From where did it come? How did it become so influential? When did the N.A.M. actually begin? These questions will be addressed in our next chapter.

Why are people becoming a part of the N.A.M., even though its belief system is so difficult to understand and so contrary to the Western mind? Three reasons help explain the phenomenon of the N.A.M.

1. It offers a religious substitute without any moral responsibility.

2. It lays a claim to revelation without any disturbing doctrine.

3. It gives an illusion of salvation without relinquishing control to a Savior.

The N.A.M.'s emphasis on power, technique, experience, immediacy and mystery helps to explain its popularity. It may also reveal that many of its adherents have merely traded in one addiction for another. "For what is a man profited if he gains the whole world, and loses or forfeits himself [his own soul]?" (Luke 9:25)

Questions for Individual Comprehension or Group Discussion

1. What aspects of the N.A.M. have you seen evident in your locality?

2. Carefully read Deuteronomy 18:9-14 and list all those practices that God finds detestable.

3. Have you unknowingly participated in a technique or practice with New Age connections? If so, have you asked God for His forgiveness?

4. What do the events in Acts 16:16-34 say to a person who believes that psychic ability is merely a latent natural ability or a gift from God? (Note verse 16: "a spirit of divination" is from the Greek *pneuma puthona*, meaning "a python spirit.")

5. In what ways could your family and your church celebrate Earth Day from a Christian perspective?[30]

6. How is 2 Timothy 3 relevant to your study of the N.A.M.?

Chapter 3

Historical Roots and Causative Factors of the New Age Movement

The N.A.M. in America did not appear out of nowhere. Its foundation has been laid, stone upon stone, over the last two centuries. The following is a brief overview of its beginnings and development in Western culture.

The Transcendental Movement

The Transcendental Movement (1836-60) was significant as the first major religious movement in America with an Asian influence. The main players were Henry David Thoreau and Ralph Waldo Emerson. Both men were deeply influenced by Eastern religious thought and held pantheistic

worldviews that were adapted to fit American individualism. They saw life's purpose as that of
transcending oneself by becoming one with nature.
Emerson also espoused the concept of the "Over-
Soul," which he defined as the mystical force in nature and in the human personality. This movement
formed a basis for what has been called the Human
Potential Movement, an informal term used to
describe a wide variety of self-help groups and ac-
tivities. The HPM is based upon the belief that
each person has an unlimited potential for change
and personal growth.

Mesmerism and New Thought

It was Austrian physician Franz Anton Mesmer
(1734-1815) who first introduced the "trance-like"
state so frequently used by New Age channelers
and psychic healers. He believed that "mesmerism," also known as "animal magnetism," was
brought about by the influence of the planets and
was therefore a completely physical phenomenon.
Mesmer's theory found its way to America in the
1830's and many began to use this hypnotic condition as a new technique for healing.

One such person was Phineas Parkhurst Quimby (1802-1866), a clock maker from Maine. He was
very disillusioned with the medical profession's
failure to diagnose and cure disease, so he set up
his own rather non-traditional medical practice.
He began to use Mesmerism as a technique to induce trance-like states in his patients and thereby
heal them. However, he came to believe that the

source of healing power was not the influence of the planets, but that which came from within the person. He called this source of power "the Mind," that spiritual part of us that is connected to God. According to Quimby, illness was not caused by disease, but rather by false belief that disturbed the healing power of the Mind.

Mary Baker Patterson Eddy, the founder of Christian Science, was one of Quimby's clients. After Quimby died, Eddy adopted many of his ideas, although she later denied Quimby's influence. She believed that sin, sickness and death were false realities and belief in them actually blocked the healing power of the Mind, the divine principle of Spirit within each person. As one understood true reality and cleared the blockage of negative thinking, then faith would release that power of the Mind to heal. It should be noted here that Eddy's understanding of faith shifted power away from God to faith itself. Faith was no longer a simple trust in God to heal one's disease, but a mental technique generated from within to heal oneself.

The Mental Healing movement eventually split into two factions after Quimby's death in 1866: Christian Science, under the leadership of Eddy (1879), and what came to be known as New Thought (in contrast to the "old thought" of traditional Christianity). These two groups shared the same worldview, but differed organizationally. The split occurred over Eddy's claim to be the original discoverer of Mental Healing. Her claim was disputed by Julius Dresser, who was also one of Quimby's original disciples and founder of the New Thought Movement.[1]

New Thought groups began to organize and in 1895, the Boston Metaphysical Club was formed. In 1899, it hosted its first Mental Healing Convention. The Club eventually evolved into the International New Thought Alliance in 1914. Its credo, full of mystical language, included "...the infinitude of the Supreme One; the Divinity of Man and his infinite possibilities through the creative power of constructive thinking and obedience to the voice of the Indwelling Presence, which is our source of Inspiration, Power, Health and Prosperity."[2] It is significant that prosperity was added to a movement that historically had healing as its main focus.

The largest modern offshoot of the New Thought movement is the Unity School of Christianity, founded in 1889 by Charles and Myrtle Fillmore.[3] Also of significance is the United Church of Religious Science begun in 1926 by Ernest Holmes. Holmes has influenced such people as Norman Vincent Peale, the popularizer of the Power of Positive Thinking, and Terry Cole-Whittaker, who started her own prosperity movement in 1982.[4]

The Christian should be suspicious of any emphasis on healing or prosperity that claims to be the result of faith operating as a scientific principle or law. Faith is not a technique or ritual for controlling God, but an attitude of trust whereby one submits to the will of God regardless of the outcome. The Bible teaches that God answers prayer on the basis of His sovereignty, wisdom, mercy and grace, not because some "law" compels Him to act. He cannot be manipulated by mind-power, positive confession or possibility thinking. Such technique-oriented manipulation of God's power is more a part of pagan magic than true religion.

Does this mean we erase from our Bibles the words of Jesus: "Your faith has made you well" (Matthew 9:22) and "Be it done to you according to your faith" (Matthew 9:29)? By no means! But we should strive to properly interpret these passages and not twist them to accommodate our fancy. Jesus "did not mean that there is some magic power triggered by believing, but that faith had opened the door for Him to heal...."[5] Therefore, faith is more an issue of relationship than technique, more a matter of whom I trust than how I think.

Spiritualism

The hypnotic trance of Mesmerism also found its way into Spiritualism with its emphasis on seances, where channelers or mediums would supposedly contact those beyond the grave.

The official beginning of Spiritualism in America occurred on the night of March 31, 1848, at the home of Margaret and Kate Fox in Hydesville, New York. The sisters, 12 and 15 years old, claimed to have established contact with a "spirit" from beyond the grave that would mysteriously rap or knock in response to certain questions (three raps for yes, one for no, two for doubtful). Thus the Fox sisters became the first "mediums" and established the practice of the seance—sitting in circles for the purpose of communicating with "spirits" who supposedly answered by raps, tilting the table or other signals.[6]

For forty years the Fox sisters traveled throughout the world, demonstrating this spirit's communication. Wherever they went, those mysterious rappings followed them. Then in 1888 the sisters confessed that it was all a fraud. They admitted to creating the rappings by snapping the joints in their toes. Margaret Fox's confession was published in the *New York Herald*, September 24, 1888, in which she said:

> I knew there was no such thing as the departed returning to this life. I have seen so much miserable deception that every morning of my life I have it before me. That is why I am willing to state that spiritualism is a fraud of the worst deception. I trust that this statement, coming solemnly from me, the first and most successful in this deception, will break the rapid growth of spiritualism and prove it is all a fraud, hypocrisy and delusion.

Unfortunately, in spite of this confession, the Spiritualist movement continued to grow in the late nineteenth and early twentieth centuries. In

1874 it was estimated that there were 11-13 million Spiritualists out of a population of 44 million Americans. Following World War I there was a resurgence of spiritualism due to the efforts of loved ones to contact those who had died in the war. How sad!

Although Spiritualism does not have the following it once did, it has served to introduce our culture to the image of the seance with its dim light, crystal ball, Ouija board and a medium making contact with the dead. Spiritualism also paved the way for various organizations to introduce occult phenomena into our culture under the aegis of the N.A.M.

One such organization is the Foundation for a Course in Miracles, originated by Kenneth and Gloria Wapnick in 1983. "The Course," which is the material the Foundation teaches, allegedly contains the wisdom of Jesus "channeled" through a woman named Helen Schucman in the early 1970's. Since that time, "The Course" has been taken by many who have seen no incompatibility between it and Christianity. Yet Kenneth Wapnick himself clearly states that the two are not compatible. "There are three basic reasons. One is the 'Course's' idea that God did not create the world. The second is the teaching that Jesus was not the only Son of God. The third involves the assertion that Jesus did not suffer and die for our sins."[7]

"The Course" is not the first nor the last bit of channeled wisdom claiming to be from Christ.[8] Beware of any such work, regardless of how Christian or biblical its claim. Upon close examination, you will always find two things present: portions of the Bible are taken out of context and reinterpreted; and the denial that Jesus is the unique, preexistent Son of God.

Theosophy (Divine Wisdom)

This movement was founded on November 17, 1875, by Col. Henry Steel Olcott (1832-1907), an officer in the Union Army, and Helena Petrovna Blavatsky (1831-91), a Russian mystic with a strong anti-Christian bias. They both were heavily involved in Spiritualism and, in fact, met at a seance. They traveled to India and added Eastern religious thought to their already existing occult beliefs. Their exposure to Asian religions laid the groundwork for much of what we see in the N.A.M. today: transcendental meditation, yoga, gurus, karma, reincarnation and teachings based on "revealed knowledge" from "Ascended Masters" (great spiritual leaders from the past who continue to channel their wisdom to our age).

Blavatsky's thought is contained in her book *The Secret Doctrine*, written in 1888. In it she claimed to have set forth the essence of all the world religions, "out of which every mystery and dogma has grown." Basically it was a presentation of the occult side of nature and religion.

After Blavatsky's death, the movement splintered. Annie Besant (1847-1933) remained in Theosophy; Alice Bailey (1880-1949) began the

Arcane School of Esoteric Philosophy; and Guy and Edna Ballard (1878-1939) founded the "I AM" movement. This latter group could also be called "the *Ascended Masters* movement." Their beliefs were based upon the gnostic theory that God is unknowable to man and can only communicate with him indirectly through dead intermediaries, known as Ascended Masters.

The Ballards' movement grew in the 1930's and 1940's by propounding the concept of the "I AM presence." This teaching offered the idea that God is within each person and that such divinity can be experienced by all who follow the purifying truth of these Ascended Masters. Since the death of the Ballards, this group has declined in its influence. However, another "I AM" group is being hailed as the fastest-growing New Age cult in the world today: The Church Universal and Triumphant, under the leadership of Elizabeth Clare Prophet. The organization originally was founded by Mark Prophet in 1958 and was known as the Summit Lighthouse. He was deeply involved in the occult when Elizabeth first met him in 1961, functioning as a medium for the Archangel Michael. He died in 1973, and became an Ascended Master. Elizabeth then became (and still is) the Living Master of the church, changing its name to The Church Universal and Triumphant in 1976.[9]

Humanistic and Transpersonal Psychology

"Transpersonal Psychology" is a branch of psychology that recognizes the need for the spiritual (transcendent) in the human experience. The spirituality that this school of thought embraces is that of Eastern pantheism and monism. The following is a brief survey of the key players in the development of this emphasis on transcendence.

Sigmund Freud (1856-1939) explored the power of the unconscious mind through a process called psychoanalysis. Sex and death became major preoccupations of his theories. People were perceived as biological creatures whose personalities were determined at an early age and whose problems were caused by repressed sexual urges or the fear of death. Freud was notoriously anti-religious, viewing God as a fabrication of one's imagination and religion itself as an illusion. Yet Freud manifested a strange attraction to the occult, psychic phenomena and fortune-tellers.

Carl Gustav Jung (1875-1961) was a student of Freud but could not agree that behavior was determined solely by biological functions. He believed that the spiritual side of the personality was a vital ingredient for mental health. In fact, he equated God with the unconscious self, the part of the self that was "older than the ego" and, therefore, closer to the "original, living spirit." He called it the Collective Unconscious, the "common substratum transcending all differences in culture and consciousness." He held to a gnostic concept that the secrets of the universe lay buried in the self and that opening oneself to one's unconscious mind would restore wholeness to the personality. Notice that by equating the God-concept with the self, Jung achieved a reconciliation of science and spirituality. Perhaps that is why psychiatry has never felt a need for religion.

Jung's father was a Protestant minister and his mother was involved in the occult. It was said that his father would often be plagued by demons banging on his study door as he prepared his sermons. Jung himself wrote a treatise entitled "The Seven Sermons to the Dead," which he claimed were dictated by spirit voices. It is not surprising to learn that Jung wrote his dissertation as a doctor of medicine on the pathology and the causes of mediumistic phenomena.

At whatever point one enters a study of the N.A.M., he or she will eventually recognize the influence of C.G. Jung. "His insights into the psyche are so universal that whether we look at gnosticism, or shamanism, or psychic phenomenon, or the individual psychology of any person, we find the profound applicability of his thought."[10]

Eric Fromm (1900-1980) was originally a Freudian psychoanalyst until he broke from that tradition in the 1930's. He rejected Freud's emphasis on the biological nature of man. He saw human nature as intrinsically good, and he attributed any evil capacity to the influence of society. He did, however, share with Freud a hostility toward Christianity, which can be clearly seen in his writings.[11] However, important for our consideration is his concept of God, "which evolved to the point that man is God; and if the sacred exists, its center is in the self and the selves of others."[12] Also, Fromm set forth five needs of the human condition that formed the basis for his therapeutic approach: the need for relatedness, the need for rootedness, the need for identity, the need for a frame of orientation and the need for *transcendence*.

Abraham Maslow (1908-1970), in his book *Motivation and Personality* (1954), placed humanity above the animal state. He chose to study the qualities of healthy people instead of those of the neurotic, and tried to discover what they were capable of and what motivated them. His "Hierarchy of Human Needs" consisted of the following levels:

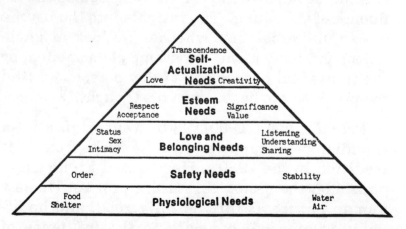

Maslow claimed that "transcendence also means to become divine or god-like, to go beyond the merely human." Maslow did not mean it in a supernatural way, but in a humanistic one. As an atheist, he preferred the terms "metahuman" or "B-human" in order to stress that this god-like potential was a part of human nature. This view was optimistic humanism at its peak. One can see how Maslow laid the psychological foundations of the Human Potential Movement and opened the door for the leap into Cosmic Humanism, which the N.A.M. has often been called.[13]

Carl Rogers (1902-1987) introduced *client-centered* therapy (as opposed to *problem-centered* therapies). It was based upon the presupposition that human nature is basically good and that, given a climate of total acceptance, it will self-actualize. Facts were quite unimportant to Rogers. What counted were the feelings that the client brought into the therapy.[14] His emphasis on experience and the autonomy of the individual self were significant.

Roger's background is an interesting study of contrast. He grew up in a highly conservative Protestant family and attended Union Theological Seminary in New York in order to prepare for the ministry. There he began to move away from the Christian faith. He writes, "My beliefs had already changed tremendously and might continue to change. It seemed to me it would be a horrible thing to have to profess a set of beliefs, in order to remain in one's profession. I wanted a field in which I could be sure my freedom of thought would not be limited."[15] In his later years, however, he delved into certain aspects of Spiritism. He attended seances with his wife in order to seek healing for her cancer. He also claimed to have contacted the spirit of his wife through a Ouija board after her death.

New Physics and Quantum Mechanics

Albert Einstein's (1879-1955) theory of relativity originally applied only to time and space. Now it has been philosophically carried over into every aspect of life. According to Einstein's theory, matter and energy are not strictly separate; all matter can be turned into energy (quanta). Einstein affirmed the theory set forth just five years earlier by Max Planck (1858-1947). Planck stated "that matter absorbed heat energy and emitted light energy discontinuously" in bursts called "energy packets," which Einstein called "quanta."[16] Thus, the relativity theory and Planck's "Quantum Mechanics" have formed the basis of a "New Physics" and have provided a scientific framework for the N.A.M. Its proponents see these theories validating the Eastern religious worldview, which believes that the basic component of the universe is spirit or energy.[17] This aspect should not be underestimated. A religious system so foreign to the Western mind has now been given credibility because it "seems" to be scientific.

The school of New Physics also uses the "uncertainty principle" (1927) of Werner Heisenberg to validate its belief in the "oneness" of all things. Heisenberg questioned the certainty of accurately measuring the movement of subatomic particles. He claimed that the very act of observation interferes with what is being studied. Thus the observer becomes a part of that which is observed. New Physics concludes that what is true on a subatomic level must also be true on a cosmic one. Everything in the universe is interconnected and nothing is independent and objective. Some would even say that the universe itself is just an extension of your reality. You are its creator and preserver. You are the "you-niverse."[18]

The following is how one physicist takes certain scientific evidence and extrapolates it philosophically:

Quantum mechanics appears to describe a universal order that includes us in a very special way. In fact, our minds may enter into nature in a way we had not imagined possible. The thought that atoms may not exist without observers of atoms is, to me, a very exciting thought. Could this fact concerning atoms also apply in other realms of science? Perhaps much of what is taken to be real is mainly determined by thought. Perhaps the appearance of the physical world is magical because the orderly processes of science fail to take the observer into account. The order of the universe may be the order of our own minds.[19]

In summary, this New Physics does not seem to be based upon good science. It starts with certain theories about the physical world and then extends them into areas of morality and spirituality, which lie outside the domain of science. Einstein's theory of relativity concerns our understanding of time and space. It should never be used to justify moral relativism.[20] Also, if there is no objective reality, then our ability to do the work of science would be totally undermined. That is why scientific discovery has flourished in cultures based upon a Judeo-Christian worldview and its emphasis on truth, reality and objectivity.[21] Without this emphasis, science is weakened.

An Invasion from the East

Those of us who grew up in the sixties will remember the invasion of Eastern religious thought through the counterculture movement. This invasion actually began in the late forties and fifties with the Beat generation or Beatniks, vets and "noncoms" from World War II whose faith in humanity had been shaken by the barbarism of the war. The Beatniks were heavily influenced by Zen Buddhism and totally disavowed a violent society; this view was reflected in their unconventional lifestyle. It centered on sensation, experience and inwardness. "Bee bop" music was "in" and one was either "hip" or "square."

The Hippie Movement

Then came the "hippies" and the protest movement of the sixties and early seventies: bells, beads, flowers, peace, love, acid—"turn on, tune in, drop out." I remember the "acid rock" of the Philmore West, the Motor City 5, the Grateful Dead, the Jefferson Airplane, the Doors, Janis Joplin, Jimi Hendrix and, of course, the Beatles. Some of us remember this last group and their love affair with India and the influence of Hinduism in their lives and music. George Harrison's "My Sweet Lord" was lip-synced by many of us until we learned it was an ode to a Hindu god (Krishna) and not to Jesus.

The popular discovery and widespread availability of such psychedelic substances as LSD and PCP became a hallmark of this particular era in American history. Their use became significant for many because of the relationship between these consciousness-altering chemicals and the experience of religious ecstasy or spirituality. Although most present New Age religious practices do not include the use of drugs, there is the same emphasis on altering consciousness in order to produce a spiritual experience.[22]

The Repeal of the Oriental Exclusion Act of 1965

There had been a steady stream of alternative religious groups into America since the 1880's, thanks to the Theosophical Society, the Unitarian Church and the Transcendentalists.[23] This stream was cut to a trickle in the early part of our century by a series of Asian immigration exclusion acts. These acts had two effects: They limited the spread of Hinduism and Buddhism, and they enabled occultist teachers to become the primary exponents of Asian wisdom, thereby solidifying the relationship between Eastern religious thought and the occult.[24]

In 1965, President Johnson lifted the ban on Asian immigration for the primary purpose of allowing refugees from Hong Kong to enter the United States. The results were astounding. Much of what we consider new on the religious scene can be traced to this open door policy to the East, from Transcendental Meditation to the Unification Church.

Occult Explosion of the Late 1960's

I have in my files a copy of *Time*, March 21, 1969, with astrologer Carroll Righter on the cover and the title, "Astrology and the New Cult of the Occult." (Mr. Righter, at that time, had been practicing astrology for thirty years and had some very famous people as clients: Marlene Dietrich, Susan Hayward, Bob Cummings, Tyrone Power, Peter Lawford and Ronald Reagan, then governor of California.)

The lead article begins by saying, "It is one of the stranger facts about the contemporary U.S. that Babylon's mystic conceptions of the universe are being taken up seriously and semiseriously by the most scientifically sophisticated generation of young adults in history. Even the more occult arts of palmistry, numerology, fortune-telling and witchcraft—traditionally the twilight zone of the undereducated and overanxious—are catching on with youngsters."

The Influence of Pierre Teilhard de Chardin

This French Jesuit priest was born in 1881, and yet his influence was not felt until the 1960's. The Catholic Church refused to allow his writings to be published until after his death in 1955. Teilhard attempted to adapt Christianity to an evolutionary worldview. He was not able to do so and still keep faith with biblical revelation. His view also failed to take sin seriously, thereby minimizing the work of Christ's redemption.

His new theology has had a great impact upon those who are in the forefront of the N.A.M. Teilhard was the name most frequently mentioned by 185 New Age leaders when asked who the most influential person was in their lives. This survey was done by Marilyn Ferguson as she was preparing her book, *The Aquarian Conspiracy.*[25]

Reading Teilhard's works is not an easy task, but one can easily see the reason his theology is so influential and appealing to those in the N.A.M. He wrote of an evolving super-humanity and urged that research and planning should take place in order to ensure its emergence. He also wrote on such themes as the cosmic Christ, the ever-growing nature of human consciousness and the development of the "noosphere," which is a layer of human consciousness that surrounds the earth's surface and enables each generation to pass on information to future generations. The most popular concept of his theology has been the "omega point," the final point of convergence when humanity will be united with itself and with God.

Human Potential Movement of the 1970's

The Human Potential Movement was based on the premise that there is more to most of us than meets the eye. It claimed that most of us have vast, unrealized potential that we must learn to tap so we can experience self-actualization and self-transcendence. (Note the connection with transpersonal psychology.) As we have mentioned, the HPM was a philosophy of self-help whereby one came to realize and utilize his unlimited capabilities.

Many groups and movements came into prominence at this time:

Esalen Institute of northern California was on the forefront of many new programs for unleashing human potential.

Transactional Analysis was a self-help method of psychiatry developed by Eric Berne (*Games People Play*, 1964), and popularized by Tom Harris (*I'm OK—You're OK*, 1968).

The Encounter Group Movement, composed of T-groups, Gestalt therapy and Creativity workshops, was designed to give a freedom of expression that leads to personal change and assertiveness.

EST (Erhard Seminars Training), is a four-day seminar designed to radically alter the way people think of themselves and of the world. Essentially *EST*, renamed *The Forum*, teaches a form of Hinduism: that the self is all there is (god).

Silva Mind Control is a technique that claims to give a person conscious control of his subconscious mind, thereby helping him to become a more productive person.

Scientology is based upon a system called Dianetics, which combines the search for one's self with Eastern religious ideas and Western scientific thought. Founded by the late L. Ron Hubbard, Scientology teaches that within all humans are uncreated gods called "Thetans," but that we must learn to discover and release the power of these beings.

Eckankar, begun by Paul Twitchell in 1964, claims to be the way by which each individual soul can become "God-realized." It is accomplished through the ancient art of Bi-Location (soul travel).

MSIA (pronounced as Messiah) is a six-day course that claims to teach an awareness of one's soul-perfection and to free one from the cycle of reincarnation.[26]

As Christians, we believe that humanity has been created in the image of God and not as gods. Our greatest potential is to be found in a person-to-person relationship with the One who made us. Our greatest tragedy is to renounce God as the center of our lives and to remain alienated from Him because of our sin. "We find ourselves only when we realize that ultimate meaning is not within us but in God our Creator, who loves us. We were made to be in relationship with him; when we acknowledge our finite, needy selves and come to him with empty, outstretched hands, he fills them fuller than we could have dreamed possible. 'I came that they might have life,' Jesus said, 'and have it abundantly' " (John 10:10).[27]

The Publication of *The Aquarian Conspiracy*

This book, written by Marilyn Ferguson and published in 1980, is known as the bible of the N.A.M. It originated from her research on the brain and consciousness. In 1975 she began publishing a bi-weekly newsletter, "Brain/Mind Bulletin." She claims that this newsletter was a "lightning rod for energy" and drew an incredible number of responses from people everywhere who shared her perspective on social change through personal transformation.

She called this movement a conspiracy: a "breathing together" of people from many professions who have seen the failures of programs and institutions that have tried to remake society by altering its outward form and organization. This conspiracy is based upon a *paradigm shift*, or a new way of thinking about old problems. This shift consists of realizing that

> human nature is neither good or bad but open to continuous transformation and transcendence. It has only to discover itself...Little wonder that these shifts of awareness are experienced as awakening, liberating, unifying, transforming. Given the

reward, it makes sense that millions have taken up such a practice within a scant few years. They discover that they don't have to wait for the world "out there" to change. Their lives and environments begin to transform as their minds are transformed.[28]

Her book is a combination of a New Age social agenda and personal vision.

The Popularization of New Age Beliefs

If Marilyn Ferguson is called the author of the New Age bible, then Shirley MacLaine could be called the High Priestess of the N.A.M.[29] Her status as a well-known Hollywood personality has provided a ready market for her books and seminars. She has done more than anyone else to popularize New Age beliefs for mainstream America. Here are some of the books that have been most widely read and eagerly received:

Out on a Limb describes Shirley MacLaine's reluctant conversion to New Age beliefs while involved in a spicy affair with a British politician. This book was also made into a five-hour television miniseries, seen by about thirty million viewers.

Dancing in the Light chronicles her further growth in the N.A.M. She describes how she came to learn about yoga, crystals, reincarnation and her many past lives.

It's All in the Playing is an account of the "ghostly" events surrounding the making of the "Out on a

Limb" television miniseries. She claims she received beyond-the-grave production assistance from the late Alfred Hitchcock and describes how weather conditions for filming were changed via visualization techniques.

Going Within is a "how to" book on meditation, visualization, color therapy, sound therapy, crystals, acupuncture and acupressure.

The New Age Messiah

In 1982, full page ads appeared in *The London Times*, *The Los Angeles Times* and *The New York Times*, stating, "The Christ Is Now Here." It indicated that Lord Maitreya (the New Age Messiah also known as a reincarnation of the Hindu god Krishna) was about to arrive and usher in the New Age. A man named Benjamin Creme, a British artist-turned-lecturer and author, was the one commissioned to announce that Maitreya was living in London waiting for the right time to make his appearance. The Tara Center is the organization that is helping the sixty-nine-year-old Creme do his "prophetic" work. This group recently (summer 1992) sponsored a conference in San Francisco, which supposedly substantiated that the World Teacher (the Christ) is already present and working powerfully in the world.

Also, in the October 1982 issue of *Reader's Digest* (p. 203), there was a full page ad sponsored by Lucis Trust. This advertized what was known as "the Great Invocation," a prayer to Maitreya. I have tried to trace the organization known as Lucis Trust by using an address contained in Constance Cumbey's book *A Planned Deception* (1985). All letters have been returned, marked "addressee unknown."

Other Causative Factors Contributing to the Rise of the N.A.M.

The failure of secular humanism. This philosophy has given us Man as the highest point on the evolutionary scale, but has also left him with no soul, with no recognition of the spiritual dimension of life.

The failure of science. The great technological advances of science have not only brought us progress, but have also brought humanity to the edge of destruction (nuclear, as well as ecological).

The failure of rugged individualism. This American philosophy of life has emphasized the individual at the expense of community, and has helped create a society of proud but lonely people.

The failure of Liberal Christianity. Biblical criticism removed the authority from God's Word by emptying the Bible of anything supernatural. The loss of the Bible's authority, in turn, emptied the faith of anything concerned with a personal relationship to God. The loss of such relationship to God narrowed the mission of the Church to issues of social justice and not to individual salvation.

The failure of Evangelical Christianity. A deficient view of the gospel (the message of Jesus Christ) has produced a spiritual concern for people, with little regard for issues of social justice. The lack of social concern has diminished the moral impact and involvement of the Church. This has created a certain societal intolerance to the Christian faith that, in turn, has pushed the Church toward greater isolation and lack of cultural involvement. Consequently, many Evangelical churches have become "fortresses" rather than "launching pads" in their failure to equip believers for ministry in an increasingly secularized culture.

Conclusion

The failures of Liberal and Evangelical Christianity provide us with both a challenge and a perspective as to how the Church must function in order to have an impact on our needy culture.

1. We must be characterized by a strong emphasis on God's communication to us through the Scriptures and through the opening up of ourselves to the Holy Spirit's power as we apply the Word to our daily lives. "All Scripture is inspired by God [God-breathed] and profitable for teaching, for reproof, for correction, for training in righteousness; that the man of God may be adequate, equipped for every good work" (2 Timothy 3:16,17).

2. We must also place a strong emphasis on establishing a person-to-person relationship

with God through Jesus Christ, based upon faith and manifesting itself through obedience. We also should encourage the expression of that intimacy through worship. "He who has My commandments and keeps them, he it is who loves Me; and he who loves Me shall be loved by My Father, and I will love him, and will disclose Myself to him" (John 14:21).

3. There should be a strong emphasis on Christian community as a place of belonging, loving and caring. Hurting and lonely people are initially attracted more to the loving environment of a church than to the orthodoxy of its doctrinal position. "A new commandment I give to you, that you love one another, even as I have loved you, that you also love one another. By this all men will know that you are My disciples, if you have love for one another" (John 13:34,35).

4. There also should be a strong emphasis on a lifestyle evangelism that shares the reality of Christ through one's "walk" as well as through one's "talk." "They profess to know God, but by their deeds they deny Him, being detestable and disobedient, and worthless for any good deed" (Titus 1:16). "And let our people also learn to engage in good deeds to meet pressing needs, that they may not be unfruitful" (Titus 3:14).

5. We must place a strong emphasis on individual regeneration (the new birth) with its
   dual manifestations of personal holiness and
   active concern for the poor and needy. "This is
   pure and undefiled religion in the sight of our
   God and Father, to visit orphans and widows
   in their distress, and to keep oneself un-
   stained by the world" (James 1:27).

6. Finally, we must learn to think "Christianly,"
   to gain a biblical worldview that enables us
   to see all of life from the perspective of the
   glory of God and the Lordship of Christ. "And
   whatever you do in word or deed, do all in the
   name of the Lord Jesus, giving thanks
   through Him to God the Father" (Colossians
   3:17).

Questions for Individual Comprehension or Group Discussion

1. Which of the historical factors discussed in this chapter do you feel has had the greatest influence on what you know to be the N.A.M.?

2. Do you think that every group that employs methods of Positive Thinking is a part of the N.A.M.? Is there a better way to identify the New Age perspective of a certain group or philosophy?

3. Are you familiar with any of the Human Potential groups mentioned in this chapter? Have you had any involvement with them that in some way is still affecting your life?

4. Can you think of any other historical antecedents or causative factors of the N.A.M. that should have been mentioned?

5. The failure of Christianity (Liberal and Evangelical) was mentioned near the end of this chapter. Which failure have you experienced the most intensely?

6. Of the solutions mentioned in the conclusion, which do you believe are the most essential?

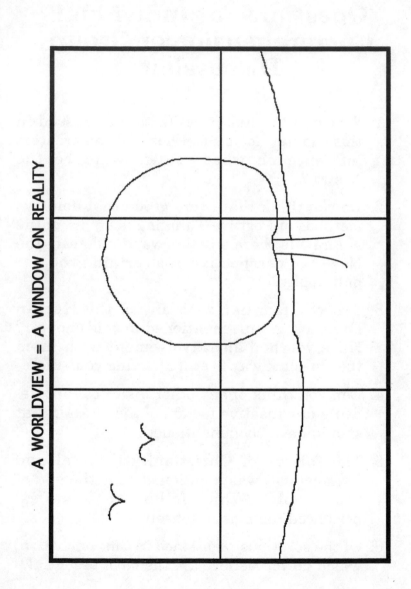

A WORLDVIEW = A WINDOW ON REALITY

Chapter 4

Worldviews

A worldview is simply a way in which we see the world; a perspective on reality that determines the way we live. It is our window on the world. (Fig. 1)

This chapter contains a comparison between the Christian and the New Age "windows." Both worldviews are compared according to the same six categories: the nature of God, the nature of Creation, the nature of Humanity, the nature of History, the nature of Truth and the nature of Reality.[1] A "grid" is included with each worldview to aid in the process of retention.

Christian (Biblical) Worldview (Fig. 2)

God is infinite and personal. The Bible declares that God is infinitely great, existing beyond our comprehension. Therefore, our knowledge of Him is not based upon human understanding or experience (He is transcendent), but on His self-revelation. He has revealed Himself as a God who is actively

CHRISTIAN (Biblical) WORLDVIEW

(Creation)   (Redemption)

Creation		Redemption
God is infinite, personal (Triune), transcendent, immanent, sovereign, good, omniscient ...	God is Creator. Cosmos was created EX NIHILO. Although God is the source of Cosmos, He did not make matter out of Himself. He SPOKE it into existence and is DISTINCT from it. Universe is orderly and open.	Humanity is created in the image of God. Dignity Significance Value Responsibility Freedom Respondability Humanity is FALLEN, the image is defaced by sin, but through the work of Christ, God is redeeming humanity.
History is linear. Creation — Fall — Redemption — Glorification Death is the gateway to eternal life or to eternal separation from God. ("Hell is a monument to human freedom" — Chesterton.)	Ethics is based on the character of God and therefore on ABSOLUTE standards revealed in the LAW.	Knowledge of reality is apprehended by faith based on reasonable evidence. God has revealed Himself: 1) nature (Rom. 1:18ff.) 2) Christ (John 1:18; Heb. 1:1-3) 3) propositional truth (Scripture) (2 Tim 3:14ff.).

engaged in His relationship to this world (He is immanent) and to humankind (He is personal). He has absolute authority over the universe (sovereignty) and yet His rulership is not one of blind determinism or fate. He is absolutely good as well as just; perfect in His love as well as in His holiness. He is revealed as having such aspects of personality as will, purpose, compassion, creativity, responsiveness, grief and wrath. He is also revealed as having such infinite characteristics as possessing complete knowledge (omniscient), unlimited power (omnipotent) and the ability to be present everywhere at all times (omnipresent). The Bible also reveals that He eternally exists as Father, Son and Holy Spirit—three distinct Persons who share the very nature of God (the Trinity).

God is Creator. The Bible reveals that this God created the material world *ex nihilo* (out of nothing) by His spoken Word. He is the Source of all creation and is also distinct from it, like an artist is distinct from his or her work. Therefore, the cosmos (universe) is not God and does not share in His essential being. Although the universe is flawed because of sin, it continues to reveal God's fingerprints.

Note the twin themes of God as *Creator* and *Redeemer* (one who frees from blame or debt) that run throughout the Bible:

Psalm 104—Creation and Providence

Psalm 105—Redemption of Israel

Revelation 4:11— "Worthy art Thou, our Lord and our God, to receive glory and honor and power; for Thou didst create all things, and because of Thy will they existed, and were created."

Revelation 5:12— "...Worthy is the Lamb that was slain to receive power and riches and wisdom and might and honor and glory and blessing."

Colossians 1:16—"For by Him [Christ] all things were created, both in the heavens and on earth, visible and invisible, whether thrones or dominions nor rulers or authorities—all things have been created through Him and for Him."

Colossians 1:13,14— "For He delivered us from the domain of darkness, and transferred us to the kingdom of His beloved Son, in whom we have redemption, the forgiveness of sins."

Humanity is created in the image of God. Humanity is a part of creation (creatureliness) and, therefore, is not part of God. Human beings are created in God's *image*, which consists of personality and spirituality, a capacity for relationship and a "respondability" to God. Man, as male and female, is created with dignity, value, freedom and significance. He is created as a material (physical) *and* a spiritual being. Humankind "fell" because of the disobedience of our primal ancestors to the absolute authority of God. They were dissatisfied with their status as finite, dependent creatures and desired a "magical" shortcut to knowledge and power. Their desire for freedom brought terrible bondage. The image was defaced through this rebellion. We ourselves are born into a spiritual exile from our Creator. We have lost the very relationship in which we are to find ultimate meaning. We continually are trying to deny the reality of this God and are striving to create our own reality. We are lost in a spiritual blindness that parades itself as a search for knowledge and power.

The solution to this exile begins with our Creator. God sent His Son to redeem sinful humanity (those who trust in Him) through His sacrificial death on the cross. Jesus Christ is the unique Son of God (only begotten), the Eternal God who took upon Himself human nature in order to redeem us. There are no spiritual techniques that we must employ in order to be brought back to God. We must simply turn from our rebellion and false reality (repentance) and receive the gift of forgiveness and restoration (faith).

Ephesians 2:1-5

> *And you were dead in your trespasses and sins, in which you formerly walked according to the course of this world, according to the prince of the power of the air, of the spirit that is now working in the sons of disobedience. Among them we too all formerly lived in the lusts of our flesh, indulging the desires of*

> *the flesh and of the mind, and were by na-*
> *ture children of wrath, even as the rest. But*
> *God, being rich in mercy, because of His*
> *great love with which He loved us, even*
> *when we were dead in our transgressions,*
> *made us alive together with Christ (by*
> *grace you have been saved).*

Colossians 1:13,14

> *For He delivered us from the domain of*
> *darkness, and transferred us to the king-*
> *dom of His beloved Son, in whom we have*
> *redemption, the forgiveness of sins.*

Human history is linear. God created time and
space as well as the physical and spiritual world.
Thus history had a distinct beginning and is
moving toward a distinct goal (creation > fall >
redemption > the new age of the Kingdom of God
ultimately revealed). History is not cyclical (it cannot be repeated) and it has meaning.

The death of an individual is also meaningful.
Death marks the end of earthly life and becomes a
gateway to either eternal life or eternal separation
from God. The determining factor is our response
to Jesus Christ.

Hebrews 9:27

> *And inasmuch as it is appointed for men to*
> *die once, and after this comes judgment.*

Revelation 20:12,15

> *And I saw the dead, the great and the*
> *small, standing before the throne, and*

books were opened; and another book was opened, which is the book of life; and the dead were judged from the things which were written in the books.... And if anyone's name was not found written in the book of life, he was thrown into the lake of fire.

Ethics is based on the character of God. We live in a moral universe where absolute standards of behavior exist. These standards are not based upon the "speculations of men" but upon the character of God. Man is not the "measure of all things," as the humanists would have us believe. God's character has been revealed in the Ten Commandments and in the law of our conscience. Therefore, there is right and wrong, truth and error, good and evil on a universal scale (a LAW above the law).

Romans 2:14-16

For when Gentiles [anyone not a Jew] who do not have the Law [Ten Commandments] do instinctively the things of the Law, these, not having the Law, are a law to themselves, in that they show the work of the Law written in their hearts, their conscience bearing witness, and their thoughts alternately accusing or else defending them, on the day when, according to my gospel, God will judge the secrets of men through Christ Jesus.

Reality is based on a personal knowledge of God. Reality is created by God and is not self-created. It is based upon the knowledge that God created both the physical and the spiritual dimensions of this world. An object is *real* because it was created by God. Reality in the physical world is discerned by our senses. However, knowledge of reality in the spiritual world is not based upon our senses or intuition, but upon a person-to-person relationship with God through faith in His Son Jesus Christ. This knowledge gives us the ability to distinguish reality from illusion.

Jeremiah 9:24

> *...let him who boasts boast of this, that he understands and knows Me, that I am the Lord who exercises lovingkindness, justice, and righteousness on earth...*

John 17:3

> *And this is eternal life, that they may know Thee, the only true God, and Jesus Christ whom Thou hast sent.*

1 Corinthians 1:18,20

> *For the word of the cross is to those who are perishing foolishness, but to us who are being saved it is the power of God ... Where is the wise man? Where is the scribe? Where is the debater of this age? Has not God made foolish the wisdom of the world?*

NEW AGE WORLDVIEW

God is an infinite, impersonal Force or Energy.	All is God; God is All.	Humanity is GOD.
PANTHEISM — reduces everything to spirit.	There are no real physical distinctions.	The problem is not sin, but ignorance.
MONISM — all existence is of one substance or essence.	Everything material is MAYA (illusion).	The chief need is change of consciousness to realize hidden divinity (AT-ONE-MENT).
	Gen. 3:5	
History is cyclical.	Truth is relative.	Reality is self-created through enlightenment.
Cosmic Evolutionary Optimism that transcends history.	There are no real distinctions between good and evil.	Knowledge vs. Faith
		Emotion vs. Reason
Reincarnation — Karma		Experience vs. Content
		Happiness vs. Obedience
Death is unreal.		The only Reality is BRAHMAN.
Gen. 3:4	Gen. 3:1	Gen. 3:6

New Age Worldview (Fig. 3)

God is infinite and impersonal. Ultimate Reality (God) is that Force or Energy that flows through everything in the universe (pantheism). All that exists is of this one essence or energy (monism). God has no characteristics or attributes of personality for it is pure energy. God, therefore, has no will; possesses no purpose; manifests no values; and encompasses both good and evil.

The universe (cosmos) is an extension of God. Whatever exists—a tree, a star, a mushroom, a person—are all an extension of the divine (pantheism). They are part of the one continuous reality, which is God. Any physical distinctions that seem to exist between people, animals, vegetables and minerals are but an illusion (maya). In other words, the material world as perceived by our senses is not real. If there is anything that is not God, and that appears to exist as a separate reality, it is illusion. The only reality is God (Brahman).

This concept of illusion is a part of Christian Science, where concepts like sin and death are believed to be unreal and where God is defined as Mind.

There is a humorous story told about Mark Twain, who once went to see a Christian Science practitioner for a reading.

"Nothing exists but Mind, eh?" he asked.
"Nothing; all else is substanceless and illusory," she replied.

"So at the end of the reading, I wrote her an imaginary check and now she is suing me for substantial dollars," said Twain.

Humanity is God. Humanity is also an extension of God, and like the rest of the universe, is essentially made "out of" God. So if God is all and all is God, then humanity is God. At the very core of existence (self or Atman) is pure energy (God or Brahman). Therefore, humanity has no definite nature, no inherent attributes, no values and no limitations.

Humans have infinite potential because they embody all the wisdom, knowledge and power of the universe. The chief problem that faces them is not *sin,* but *ignorance* of their divine status. Any separation or barrier that they experience from God is due to incorrect perceptions imposed by society or religions that teach such concepts as reason and faith. Jesus was a man who realized His divinity and became the Christ. He is a "Way-shower" for humanity so that they too might become "Christs."

Swami Muktananda said, "Kneel to your own self, honor and worship your own being. God dwells within you as You."[2]

Marharishi Mahesh Yogi urges his followers to "be still and know that YOU are God."[3]

This is the chief message one receives from reading *Out on a Limb* by Shirley MacLaine. She stood on the seashore at Malibu Beach, stretched out her arms and yelled, "I am God!" In her book *Dancing in the Light,* she writes, "I know that I exist, therefore *I AM.* I know the God-source exists, therefore *It Is.* Since I am part of that force, then *I AM that I AM"* [emphasis mine].[4]

Werner Erhard, in his training sessions called EST (renamed The Forum), says that "all is perfect; we just don't see it that way. Humans are not depraved or dependent on any outside source of deliverance or strength. The answer is not reconciliation with a God different from ourselves, but the realization that we ourselves are God. The self is the cosmic treasury of wisdom, power and delight...we make our own rules."[5]

Elizabeth Clare Prophet is presently the leader in The Church Universal and Triumphant, the fastest growing New Age cult in the world. The following is a portion of a speech she gave in 1990 at the Conference on Spiritual Freedom in Los Angeles, which I recorded:

"Gnosticism is a path of self-realization. Jesus also walked it." That statement is blasphemy to orthodoxy because they want you to believe He was born a flesh and blood God...and since you weren't born a flesh and blood God, you could not possibly ever equate with the path, or the mission, or the discipleship of Jesus Christ. Because He was a different kind of being, an exception, He was not like the rest of us sinners, and there is no hope for us except to latch onto His coattails. This affirmation of the flesh and blood God has denied to every Christian since, the role of Christ. And this is why Jesus wept....

Hence yoga, TM and other less familiar programs are designed to raise one's consciousness of who one truly is. In New Age jargon, this process of realization is called *at-one-ment*. This distinctly Christian term, meaning reconciliation with God through the death of Jesus Christ, is now used to describe a reconciliation with one's own divinity.

History is cyclical. History is like a river that flows into the ocean whose water evaporates into the atmosphere and comes down again into the river as rain. Time is illusory and history has no final meaning. The ultimate purpose of life is to transcend history in the soul's journey back to God. The death of a person is of no consequence because the soul (Atman, the self contained within the person) is indestructible. This soul enters another body and begins a new lifetime in its flow toward God (the process called Transmigration of the Soul, better known as Reincarnation). These multiple lifetimes provide many chances for the soul to pursue its transcendence (164 chances in classic Hinduism). The circumstances of one's "rebirth" are determined by the sum total of one's good and bad actions in a previous lifetime (Karma). These bad actions (although illusory) cannot be confessed or forgiven. They must be worked out alone.

Most popular Western versions of reincarnation involve a transmigration of the soul into other human forms. But most Eastern religions do not distinguish between human, animal, vegetable or mineral forms of existence.[6]

Truth is relative. Good and evil, right and wrong, truth and error are all arbitrary distinctions. God is beyond such distinctions and cannot be limited by them. Since humanity is God, it too is beyond the limitations of values and rules.

An example from the *Star Wars* trilogy may help to illustrate this point. Luke Skywalker, who is the representative of all that is good, turns out to be none other than the son of Darth Vader, the representative of the dark side. They become reconciled at the end of the story and their "oneness" is underscored.

Another illustration can be found in the movie *Dark Crystal*. When the lost chard from the crystal is found, the unity of the crystal is restored and the Mystics (good) and the Skecsees (evil) are fused into one. Evil is just the dark side of the good.

Compare these modern illustrations with this quote from the Buddha: "Therefore it seems to me that everything that exists is good—death as well as life, sin as well as holiness, wisdom as well as folly."[7]

Reality is self-created through enlightenment. Reality is not something known by content or faith, but through self-realization (enlightenment). As humanity becomes aware of its divinity it will begin to exercise the power to create reality. Thus humans escape the illusion of the world as they "see" it, either by moving into an altered state of consciousness or by choosing their own reality through the power of the mind. Visualization (directed imagination) is based upon the "god-like" ability to control reality: I am God, I have the power to create with my mind what I choose to exist. My friend sitting next to me exists because I have chosen him to be a part of my reality.

> Pure monism at its fundamental level believes that all there is, all one can know, see and experience is simply a projection of the Self. The solitary individual is the final definitive Self of the cosmos and all other individuals are mere projections... There is only One... The final John Doe of pure monism is all there really is, making the Fred Smiths of the world merely his visualized projections.[8]

The underlying purpose of visualization, therefore, is to control one's circumstances and existence.[9]

Thus, within the N.A.M., a content-oriented faith that limits one's reality must be swept away. That is the reason, in this movement:

> *Knowledge* (*gnosis*—enlightenment) is more important than *Faith*;
> *Feelings* are more important than *Reason*;
> *Experience* (right hemisphere of the brain) is more important than *Content* (left hemisphere); and

Personal Happiness is more important than *Obedience or Service,* which have led some to describe the N.A.M. as a religion of narcissism.

Conclusion

If we look at satan's temptation in the Garden of Eden, we will notice the first evidence of the New Age worldview. Again we see that the N.A.M. is not very new at all, but the repackaging and modernizing of the oldest lies in human history. These lies have now moved west of Eden and are affecting the very basis of Western thought and culture.

Genesis 3:1-6

Now the serpent was more crafty than any beast of the field which the Lord God had made. And he said to the woman, "Indeed, has God said [questioning of absolute truth], *'You shall not eat from any tree of the garden'?" And the woman said to the serpent, "From the fruit of the trees of the garden we may eat; but from the tree which is in the middle of the garden, God has said, 'You shall not eat from it or touch it, lest you die.' " And the serpent said to the woman, "You surely shall not die* [denial of death]*! For God knows that in the day you eat from it your eyes will be opened* [promise of enlightenment], *and you will be like God* [self-deification], *knowing good and evil." When the woman saw that* *the tree was good for food* [personal happiness], *and that it was a delight to the eyes* [experience-centered], *and that the tree was desirable to make one wise* [knowledge is power], *she took from its fruit and ate; and she gave also to her husband with her, and he ate.*

Questions for Individual Comprehension or Group Discussion

1. Can you clearly compare the worldview of the New Age with that of biblical Christianity? Work on a comparison.

2. Think through your own worldview and ask, "Am I living consistently within this window, or am I borrowing from other perspectives and inventing my own?" (That is syncretism.)

3. What impact would the N.A.M.'s view of ethics have upon our culture if applied consistently?

4. Why do you think karma is an inconsistency within the New Age system?

5. What experience, if any, have you had with visualization? Do you think that such a practice can exist within a biblical perspective? (Be sure to read the Appendix to Chapter 6.)

6. Can you find a place within Christianity for reincarnation? Why or why not?

Chapter 5

Evaluation of the
New Age Movement

Part One—Points of Agreement

The basic presupposition that I use to evaluate divergent belief systems is: *all truth is God's truth.* Whatever I see and wherever I see that which is true, honorable, right, pure, holy, of good repute, excellent and worthy of praise, I should let my mind dwell on those things (Philippians 4:8).

What I am saying is that wherever there is truth—no matter where it is found—we should see it as God's truth for it is His world and "His invisible attributes, His eternal power and divine nature, [can be] clearly seen, being understood through what has been made..." (Romans 1:20) Satan is the master of the half-truth, around which he builds a whole deceptive system of thought that is designed to lead a seeker away from the truth.

We may see the truth of God within even such a system. If so, we must recognize it as such and use it as a means of leading the seeker to the whole truth.

Our evaluation of the N.A.M. begins with some truths with which Christians can find agreement. As you engage the New Age person in conversation, these points can form the basis of a constructive dialogue and an opening for the points of disagreement, which will be discussed in the next chapter.

Stewardship of Creation. A distinctive of the N.A.M. is its desire to protect the environment rather than exploit it. Christians need to understand that the mandate given by God to humankind in Genesis 1:26-30 was one of responsible stewardship rather than one of self-centered dominance. He gave us this earth that we might care for it and, in return, that it might sustain us. Our active involvement in issues relating to conservation and the environment should not be motivated by a reverence for the earth, but by obedience to its Creator. If creation is a way by which God's glory is revealed (Psalm 19:1; Romans 1:20), then we who desire to declare the glory of God should strive to be good caretakers of His handiwork. (See discussion question 5 for Chapter 2 on page 38 and the related endnote.)

Emphasis on Peace. Jesus said, "Blessed are the peacemakers, for they shall be called sons of God" (Matthew 5:9). Christians may have differing viewpoints on national defense, but peace and reconciliation between individuals and nations are a part of God's truth. In fact, peacemaking is a characteristic of belonging to God's family. In saying this, we must also recognize that all earthly peace is fragile and temporary without the Lordship of Jesus Christ, the Prince of Peace, and that lasting peace will not be known until the "New Age" of God's Kingdom is revealed.

Stewardship of the Human Body. Our bodies have been created by God and are temples of the Holy Spirit (Genesis 2:7; 1 Corinthians 6:19-20). Therefore, like those within the New Age, we should be concerned with proper exercise, good nutrition and healthy habits as well as with the disciplines of the soul (1 Timothy 4:7,8). Christians have been affected more by the Greek concept of a body/spirit distinction than by the Hebrew model of a body/spirit unity. This latter perspective sees humankind as physical and spiritual beings. The Bible recognizes that the human body is weak and frail and even that it is the repository for sinful habits and desires. However, we cannot conclude that the Bible views the body or the concerns of the body as being inherently evil. Christ's redemption of the believer includes the resurrection of his body from the dead. St. Paul said, "So also is the resurrection of the dead. It is sown [buried] a perishable body, it is raised an imperishable body" (1 Corinthians 15:42).[1]

Encouragement of Creativity and the Use of Imagination. The N.A.M., because of its emphasis upon experience, encourages the use of imagination and creativity. Many New Age leaders encourage their students to develop a "right-brain" kind of thinking. The right hemisphere of the brain is where creative thinking takes place, in contrast to the logical thinking of the left hemisphere, which more often is valued by our culture. Although this split-brain theory is overstated (recent research indicates considerable overlapping and cooperation of the two hemispheres), Christians can agree that the use of our creativity and imagination for the glory of God should be encouraged.

Our heavenly Father is the Artist who created all things and He has made creativity a part of His image in us. Too often the Christian Church has validated more traditional forms of ministry, such as pastoral or missionary work, and has not encouraged vocations in the arts and culture. When art has been encouraged, for example, it is limited in many Christian circles to religious symbols and moralistic messages instead of being given the freedom to express all of life to the glory of God. "Art is an expression of who we are and is an appropriate response to a God who requires that we give all that we are to him."[2]

We need to pray for more Christians to recognize and value their gifts of creativity and imagination. We need to pray that they would start developing their gifts to write, paint, draw, sculpt, dance, conduct or perform for the glory of God. We also need to pray that they not fall into the trap of making an idol out of their creativity, but that they use their gifts to express who they are in relationship to the Creator of us all.

Recognition of a World Vision. The N.A.M. emphasizes a type of global thinking that sees the earth as a unified and interrelated system rather than as a world of diversity. The biblical perspective is also a global one. Although God's revelation to humankind is very specific, its application is universal. God said to His Messiah, "It is too small a thing that You should be My Servant to raise up the tribes of Jacob, and to restore the preserved ones of Israel; I will also make You a light of the nations so that My salvation may reach to the end of the earth" (Isaiah 49:6). Although salvation is centered upon faith in Jesus Christ alone, it is open to those of every race and culture. The apostle Peter, quoting an Old Testament passage, said, "And it shall be, that every one who calls on the name of the Lord shall be saved" (Acts 2:21).

If we are to share God's vision for the world, we must see to it that our lifestyles reflect the simplicity of Christ. We must realize that preoccupation with our own well-being not only blurs our vision of a needy world but also hinders us from stepping out of our comfort zones in order to meet those needs.

Emphasis on Unity and Cooperation. There is an emphasis among those in the N.A.M. upon cooperation and networking. They have an understanding that only through working together will the world be transformed. The Bible also says that our impact upon the world will flow out of unity and love for one another in the Church. Jesus said to His disciples, "By this all men will know that you are My disciples, if you have love for one another" (John 13:35). Jesus even prayed "...that they may be one, just as We are one; I in them, Thou in Me, that they may be perfected in unity, that the world may know that Thou didst send Me, and didst love them, even as Thou didst love Me" (John 17:22,23).

How are we doing in this regard? Very often disharmony and unresolved conflict in a church or ministry may lead the unbelieving world to doubt the reality of a living Christ. Competition and ambition often prevent us from serving each other and considering others more highly than we do ourselves (see Philippians 2:4). Even though we know that unity does not mean unanimity and that there will always be disagreement in the Church, we must strive to outdo one another in deference and respect. We also must take the words of Jesus seriously, that "whoever wishes to become great among you shall be your servant, and whoever wishes to be first among you shall be your slave; just as the Son of Man did not come to be served, but to serve, and to give His life a ransom for many" (Matthew 20:26-28).

Realization of a World Gone Wrong. The N.A.M. points out that something is desperately wrong with our world that only a radical transformation of humanity can rectify. Christianity certainly agrees with this realization.

The Bible describes the human condition in the following way: "There is none righteous, not even one; there is none who understands, there is none who seeks for God; all have turned aside, together they have become useless; there is none who does good, there is not even one. Their throat is an open grave, with their tongues they keep deceiving, the poison of asps is under their lips; whose mouth is full of cursing and bitterness; their feet are swift to shed blood, destruction and misery are in their paths, and the path of peace have they not known. There is no fear of God before their eyes" (Romans 3:10-18). People need to be "born again." That does not mean to be reincarnated, but to be given a new nature or capacity for relationship with God that changes a person from the inside out (John 3:1-17). This authentic change in the human heart is possible only through faith in Jesus Christ, who also works through the believer to be "salt" and "light" in society (Matthew 5:13-16).[3]

Sociologist Jeremy Rifkin in his book, *The Emerging Order: God in the Age of Scarcity*, comes to a very interesting conclusion about the world economic crisis. He believes that change in a world gone wrong is possible through one of two ways: either through a one-world government like the N.A.M. envisions or through a spiritual revival along the lines of a Charismatic/Evangelical kind.[4]

Emphasis on Holism in Medicine. The N.A.M. has correctly taken Western medical science to task for functioning primarily with a mind/body separation and failing to recognize the place of the spiritual in the process of recovery. The Scriptures recognize the impact of stress, anxiety, anger, bitterness, fear and guilt upon the body as well as upon the mind. "A joyful heart is good medicine, but a broken spirit dries up the bones" (Proverbs 17:22). "Hope deferred makes the heart sick, but desire fulfilled [coming] is a tree of life" (Proverbs 13:12). "The fear of the Lord prolongs life, but the years of the wicked will be shortened" (Proverbs 10:27). "When I kept silent about my sin, my body wasted away...my vitality was drained away as with the fever-heat of summer. I acknowledged my sin to Thee...And Thou didst forgive the guilt of my sin" (Psalm 32:3-5).

Therefore, it should not surprise us to see evidence that attitudes and emotions are linked to our immune systems. Certain emotions cause the brain to release chemical messengers called *neuropeptides* which affect the production of white blood cells when infection is present. We also know that the body, upon stimulation, releases a certain substance known as *endorphins*. These are natural chemicals in the brain, spinal cord and other tissues that are similar in structure to opiates and heroin and that function as a natural anesthetic for pain as well as a part of the body's immune system. In fact, studies at the National Institute for Mental Health have shown that acupuncture needles may cause the body to produce endorphins, which would explain the reason for this treatment being successful in some cases.[5]

If you see or hear of a medical practice that you think is suspicious, ask three questions: 1) Is there scientific evidence that this practice works? 2) What is the origin of this practice? 3) Upon what worldview is this practice based? If you detect an Eastern religious perspective by which healing is *said* to be accomplished through the "energy" flow or "life force" of the body, do not expose yourself to such a practice. Desperation and a lack of discernment have driven many a Christian to occult practices rather than to the God who heals.[6]

The Centrality of the Spiritual. Christians should heartily agree with the fact that "man is incurably religious" and that the most precious issues of life are of a spiritual nature. "Do not lay up for yourselves treasures upon earth, where moth and rust destroy, and where thieves break in and steal. But lay up for yourselves treasures in heaven, where neither moth nor rust destroys, and where thieves do not break in or steal" (Matthew 6:19,20).

Spirituality, however, needs to be focused and carefully defined. "Now we have received, not the spirit of the world, but the Spirit who is from God, that we might know the things freely given to us by God" (1 Corinthians 2:12). If we indiscriminately open ourselves up to the spiritual realm, we may be confronted by a cosmic array of evil forces (see Ephesians 6:12). Consequently, it is a realm in which there is much spiritual deception and danger. "But the Spirit explicitly says that in later times some will fall away from the faith, paying attention to deceitful spirits and doctrines of demons" (1 Timothy 4:1).

The greatest instrument we have to help us navigate these treacherous waters is the truth of God's Word, the Bible. Jesus said to the Father, "Thy word is truth" (John 17:17). Although the truth that is contained in the Scriptures and in Jesus Christ may seem narrow to our "tolerant" culture, it is the only way that leads to eternal life. Jesus also said, "I am the way, and the truth, and the life; no one comes to the Father, but through Me" (John 14:6).

Conclusion

These nine ideas are important because they form various points of contact with those who are in the N.A.M. Such points are necessary in order to form a bridge to those with whom we seek to share our faith. In Chapter 7 we will see how the apostle Paul used such an approach with the Athenians in Acts 17 to pave the way for sharing the distinctives of the Christian faith.

The questions for Chapter 5 are combined with the questions for Chapter 6. Please interact with these questions after reading Chapter 6.

Chapter 6

Evaluation of the New Age Movement

Part Two—Points of Disagreement

The following are the main points of disagreement between Christianity and the N.A.M. Notice how each corresponds to the six "windowpanes" of the worldview windows in Chapter 4.

The Nature of God. The Bible teaches that God is both infinite and personal, the Ever-Unknowable and the Ever-Knowable. The N.A.M. defines its God as infinite and impersonal—merely a Force or Energy. Therefore, no such concept as a personal relationship with God can exist within its system since pantheism presupposes an impersonal deity. Such a God cannot show mercy, love or grace. How can our New Age friends consider the belief in Perfect Nothingness (Nirvana) a step forward in their search for the true God?

The Nature of Nature. The Bible teaches that nature (cosmos) is created and yet distinct from the Creator. The N.A.M. is *pantheistic* in that it views nature as an extension of the divine. Such a worldview has begotten a generalized belief in Gaia, the goddess concept of Earth, and birthed a whole set of ecological groups who are religiously motivated in their care of the planet.

C. S. Lewis once said, "Pantheism is a creed not so much false as hopelessly behind the times. Once, before creation, it would have been true to say that everything was God. But [then] God created: He caused all things to be other than Himself."[1]

Pantheism, which claims no distinctions within nature, does not increase the value of human life. Rather, it devalues life by deifying nature. When God is not God, man is not man. If God is not properly exalted, man will not be given his rightful place in the universe, created "a little lower than God [the angels], and [crowned] with glory and majesty" (Psalm 8:5). Instead, the New Age man or woman becomes depersonalized and is of no more value than an animal. "For even though they knew God, they did not honor Him as God, or give thanks; but they became futile in their speculations, and their foolish heart was darkened. Professing to be wise, they became fools, and exchanged the glory of the incorruptible God for an image in the form of corruptible man and of birds and four-footed animals and crawling creatures" (Romans 1:21-23).

If everything is one continuous reality and there is no distinction between humans and animals, then could cows and rats ever become just as sacred as certain people? Isn't this what we see in India, a nation that has had a pantheistic worldview for millennia?

We are seeing the devaluation of human life in our country as well. A person who kills or damages a bald eagle, its egg or nest is subject to a fine of up to $5,000 or imprisonment for up to a year *(U.S. Code, Title 16, Section 668)*. However, there is no legal penalty for aborting an unborn child.

The Nature of Humanity. The Bible teaches that humanity was created in the *image of God*, therefore with inherent dignity and significance. Man fell from that high estate through sinful rebellion. God made provision for our restoration through the sacrificial death of Jesus Christ, the God-Man, who came to seek and to save the lost (see Luke 19:9,10).

In contrast, the N.A.M. believes that humanity "appeared" through the evolutionary process and shares divinity in common with all of nature. To the N.A.M., therefore, humanity's problem is not sin, but ignorance of its true identity. So the solution is not redemption but enlightenment.

According to Elizabeth Clare Prophet, "Many Gnostics have said that ignorance, not sin, is what involves a person in suffering. You are not sinners, you are merely not awake. So stop thinking of yourself as a sinner, because while you are beset with that self-condemnation, you are turning aside from the real issue...It is a doctrine of satan that tells you that you are sinners."[2]

Christianity may be faulted with much, historically speaking, but not that it fails to take evil seriously. The N.A.M. suffers from a moral unreality. It does not deal realistically with the world's pain and suffering. It tends toward self-centeredness and escapism by offering a desperate world "Peace" when there is none. "And they have healed the [brokenness] of My people [superficially], saying, 'Peace, peace,' but there is no peace" (Jeremiah 6:14). Also, the law of *karma* only postpones and thereby perpetuates the problem of evil rather than confronting it squarely and offering a solution. Such a law also cheapens human life by viewing one's present suffering as the result of evil done in a past life (bad karma), thereby cultivating a lack of societal compassion. Why should anyone give to the poor if their condition is due to the evil and irresponsibility of their past lives?

The N.A.M. also borrows from ancient Gnosticism when it makes a distinction between Jesus and the Christ, by teaching that Jesus was a man who perfected Himself to a level where He *became* the Christ, something of which we all are capable. This excerpt from a New Age journal makes this idea clear:

The institutional Christian churches tell us that Jesus was the only Son of God, that he incarnated as a human in order to die on the cross as a penalty for our sins...But, that is a sad caricature...It turns Jesus into a magical fairy-tale hero and Christianity into a degenerate cult of personality...Jesus did not 'save' people; he freed them—from the bondage of ego. The significance of incarnation and resurrection is not that Jesus was a human like us but rather that we are gods like him—or at least have the potential to be.[3]

Where in the Bible does it say that one can become the Christ? Why are we told instead that it was Jesus Christ who created the universe (1 Corinthians 8:6; Colossians 1:16)? Why does the New Testament also state that the only Mediator between God and humanity is not our "Christ-self," but the Man, Christ Jesus (1 Timothy 2:5)? Why does the Bible declare that "there is salvation in no one else; for there is no other name under heaven that has been given among men, by which we must be saved" (Acts 4:12)?

"Who is the liar but the one who denies that Jesus is the Christ? This is the antichrist, the one who denies the Father and the Son" (1 John 2:22; see also verse 23).

The Nature of History. The Bible teaches that history has a beginning and is moving toward an appointed goal: the new age of the Kingdom of God. Death is real and final, the result of human sin. The N.A.M. believes in a cyclical history that has no real meaning or purpose. Death is essentially denied in reincarnation. As Helen Wambach said in one of her lectures, "The Age of Aquarius means that we're learning that we never die. You will experience many lives, many time periods."[4]

Why? The law of karma is inexorable. No one lifetime is long enough to work out of the "black hole" of one's "bad karma." Thus reincarnation becomes the ultimate method of self-salvation. How many lifetimes will this self-atonement take? Can one be sure of achieving it? Then what? Who is it that holds the power of karma over us if we are gods and all the world is an extension of our reality?

The Bible declares that salvation does not come through the working out of one's karma, but by the grace of God: "For by grace you have been saved through faith; and that not of yourselves, it is the gift of God: not as a result of works, that no one should boast" (Ephesians 2:8,9). Thus God has graciously declared us forgiven through our faith in what Jesus Christ has done for us on the cross when He took all our "bad karma" upon Himself. He also has given us the certainty of resurrection unto an eternal life of unhindered and ever-growing relationship to Himself (see John 14:1-3).

The Nature of Truth. The Bible teaches the existence of "Truth" based upon the absolutes of God's Law; that there is right and wrong, good and evil, and that they are distinct and opposite. The N.A.M. teaches an ethical relativity based on philosophical monism. There is not only "truth for me" but also "truth for you." These can exist at the same time without contradiction.

Shirley MacLaine says, "Evil is just the word *live* spelled backwards...just a lower form of consciousness."[5] James Bjornstad, a New Testament professor at King's College, tells of a talk show he was on with MacLaine, where she claimed that she had gained a new perspective on rape. She believes that men who rape women are probably their lovers from previous lives. MacLaine also excused her adulterous relationship with a married man after she was told by a channeler that she and this man were married in a previous life.[6] In the same seance, she was told that homosexuality can be easily explained as a rocky sexual transition from a prior life.[7]

It is this point that should concern us most about the N.A.M.: If reality (God) is both good and bad (*yang* and *yin*), then we are free to copy either side of God's nature. For example, the spirit guide Ramtha, a 35,000-year-old warrior from the "lost continent" of Atlantis channeled through J.Z. Knight, has said, "Every vile, wretched thing you do broadens your understanding...if you want to do anything, regardless of what it is, it would not be wise to go against that feeling; for there is an experience awaiting you and a good adventure that will make your life sweeter."[8]

Is it possible to live out a life of ethical relativity? Is there really no difference between cruelty and kindness? Is there not something that registers within us, whether an action is right or wrong? What explains our sense of guilt and our sense of justice? Are they merely a matter of cultural conditioning?

The Nature of Reality. Christianity says that what we know to be true and real has been created by God. This infinite God has chosen to reveal Himself personally to us in His Son Jesus Christ. Thus, when we enter into a person-to-person relationship with the Creator, we have a framework in which to discern truth from error and reality from illusion. The N.A.M. believes that reality is self-created—since we are considered deity, we are told that we have the power to create our own reality. This idea is what most visualization techniques are based upon: the power of the mind to bring into reality whatever it imagines.[9]

Yet the sword cuts both ways on this one. The idea that a person is totally responsible for his own reality is the dark side of the N.A.M. There are some who teach that the Jews themselves brought on the Holocaust; that some minorities have created their own ghettos; that rape victims brought this tragedy on themselves subconsciously; that the sick are responsible for their own infirmities.

Certainly God has given us a power of choice and our choices help create the reality in which we live. But the fly in the New Age ointment is that mind-power supplants faith in God, and whenever one eliminates God, bondage will follow. Therefore, one cannot suffer or face tragedy without the horrible awareness that he has brought those things upon himself.

What an interesting way satan has designed for shifting the responsibility for his evil tactics onto poor struggling humanity; and all for the small price of allowing people to think they are gods! *If we are deity, and all the world is just an extension of our reality, then why have we not created a perfect one?!*

Conclusion

In these last three chapters, I have sought to provide a framework in which the belief system of the N.A.M. could be compared with that of Christianity. It is hoped, however, that the reader will have gained far more than information. This material has also been written to help the Christian understand points of agreement and disagreement with the N.A.M. so as to more effectively share with these people the Good News about Jesus Christ. The major focus of my last chapter is on becoming a more effective witness to those in the N.A.M.

Questions for Individual Comprehension or Group Discussion
(on Chapters 5 and 6)

1. Do you agree with the author's statement that "all truth is God's truth?" What are the limitations of such a statement?

2. Can you remember at least five points of agreement between Christianity and the N.A.M.?

3. You will notice that the six points of disagreement between Christianity and the N.A.M. correspond to the six panes of the worldview windows in the previous chapter. Which point do you feel is the most significant of all?

4. Develop a few questions that you would be able to ask someone in the N.A.M. concerning the point of disagreement you chose in question 3. Make sure your questions do not attack the person, but help the person see the inconsistency of his/her position.

5. Study 1 John 4:1-6 and list the ways this passage deals with the issues we have addressed in this chapter.

Chapter 7

Hints on Relating to Those in the N.A.M.

Sharing our faith in Jesus Christ with those in the N.A.M. is a challenge as well as a responsibility. The following are suggestions that will help you be more effective in your witness.

1. Remember that you are dealing with *people* who hold New Age beliefs and not the demon-possessed or aliens from outer space (although they probably believe in them). These are people who are searching for spiritual truth and who have a soul-hunger for meaning. They have seen that technological advances, humanistic psychology, drugs, relationships and materialism have failed to bring peace and healing to their troubled lives. In many respects, they are fulfilling the search that God ordained when

He etched within His creation a desire for Himself, "that they should seek God, if perhaps they might grope for Him and find Him, though He is not far from each one of us" (Acts 17:27). Respect and tolerance are very important to people in the N.A.M.

2. Strive to establish points of contact with them, perhaps by looking for areas of agreement with their system (see Chapter 5). Look for ways to affirm them and their search for truth.

Paul gives us a pattern for this approach in Acts 17. He was moved to speak to the Athenians because he saw the glory of God being diminished by idolatry (v. 16). "The glory of God, not the needs of the unreached, should be the driving force of the Church's mission" (Johannes Verkel). We, like Paul, should be motivated to speak to those in the N.A.M. because the glory of God is being diminished by their false belief system.

Paul sought a point of commonality and affirmation (v. 22). "I see that you are very religious." This reminds me of an interesting story once told by Paul Little, who at that time was Director of Evangelism for Inter-Varsity Christian Fellowship: An evangelist boarded a train and was delighted to see an empty car. Such a situation would afford him the time and peace he needed before his next speaking engagement. Just before the train was about to move, a "drunk" came into the car. Swaggering down the aisle, he chose to plop himself down next to the preacher, though there was a sea of empty seats. He proceeded to offer a drink to his new seatmate. The evangelist, resisting the urge to condemn, responded this way: "No, thank you, but I see you are a very generous man." The drunk man was touched with such a kind remark and began to cry. The evangelist led him to Christ by the end of the trip.

The apostle Paul found such a point of commonality, a recognition of the Athenians' religious search and their fears, to lead them to a further understanding of God (v. 23). Certainly, the New Age God is the "Unknown God"—"the Ever-Unknowable"—and we, like Paul, have a chance to make Him known in Jesus Christ.

Paul also demonstrated a familiarity with the philosophical-religious system of the Athenians. He even quoted one of their poets and skillfully appealed to both the Epicurean and the Stoic perspectives (vv. 24-28). So we should be conversant with the worldview of those to whom we witness.

He did not have an overwhelming response, but those converts he made (Dionysius and Damaris) were significant (v. 34). Be prepared for a long process when sharing with those who hold New Age beliefs. You may not have many come to Christ, but those who do may be significant ones who will have great influence on others.

3. Define your terms; realize that the N.A.M. uses biblical language *with different meaning*. Here are some examples of the New Age use of familiar terms:[1]

Born Again—"Dying to the past and the old sense of self through a change in consciousness."

Sin—"To 'miss the mark' of God-Consciousness."

Repentance—"Going beyond or higher than the ordinary mental state;" transcending a self-centered ego and becoming God-centered.

Conversion—"A transformation of self based on a new state of awareness...a higher consciousness."

Jesus Christ—"Jesus was an historical person who lived 2,000 years ago...The significance of Jesus, therefore, is not as a vehicle of salvation but as a model of perfection. That is why the proper attitude toward him is one of reverence, not worship. Jesus showed us the way to a higher state of being and called us to realize it...individually and as a race."

"Christ...is a title...conventionally translated as 'anointed', it really means 'perfected' or 'enlightened' or 'the ideal form of humanity'...

an eternal transpersonal condition of being to which we must all someday come."

The Second Coming—"Waking up from the illusion of ego, from the dream of worldly life, into God...the final appearance of Christ will be a worldwide *spiritual* appearance, free from all physical limitations."

Salvation—"...as liberation or enlightenment is possible for us at every moment."

4. Tell them your concern that they are leaving themselves open to danger and deception. Point out that the Bible acknowledges the operation of spiritual powers, of both good and evil, and warns against involvement in the occult. Use the following passages:

Leviticus 19:31; 20:6; Deuteronomy 18:9-13; 1 Samuel 28:1-19; Isaiah 8:19-20; 47:8-15; Ezekiel 28:2-10; Luke 8:26-39; Acts 16:16-21; and Revelation 22:15.

You can even use the warnings of those involved in the N.A.M. "Yoga is not a trifling jest if we consider that any misunderstanding in the practice of Yoga can mean death or insanity."[2]

Practitioners of *yoga* warn of the power of *Kundalini* energy, represented as a serpent coiled at the base of the spine. The purpose of many forms of yoga is to awaken the *Kundalini* and to release its energies upwards through the seven "chakras" (energy centers of the body). But yogis say it is dangerous, for one might get burned from the serpent's hot breath—or go insane.[3] In fact, much has been written about the subject of "transpersonal emergencies," (a state of shock) which often occur during the use of various consciousness-raising techniques.[4]

An article in *Yoga Journal* on parapsychology even warns the seeker that the use of such phenomena as Ouija boards, automatic writing and other means of divination "in a frivolous and disrespectful manner" makes one "liable to attract lower disincarnate communicators, including ghosts and poltergeists, and makes one run the risk of becoming obsessed or possessed."[5]

5. Challenge their assumptions. Question your friends about their beliefs and practices. Doing so will serve two purposes: It will show your interest and it will get them to think, without putting them on the defensive, about some of the inconsistencies and *non sequiturs* that they may see but are unwilling to admit. For example:

How do you know that?

What evidence do you have for that?

If everything is truly relative, how could we live in such a world? How can a human society function without any absolutes?

Isn't there something in you that knows a particular act is wrong in and of itself? From where does that consciousness come?

Can pantheism form an adequate moral basis for culture?

6. Point out inconsistencies. India has had a "New Age" worldview for thousands of years and should have long ago eliminated hunger, violence, overpopulation and racism. Why hasn't it? Could it be that the solution to these problems does not lie in paradigm shifts or transformations of consciousness, but in salvation from the sinfulness and self-ishness of the human heart?

Why is it that every scientific study that has been done on horoscopes has proven that they "fail completely in predicting future events"?[6]

One can also stress the fact that the nature of faith presupposes that it have a *reliable object*. Something does not become true just because you believe in it hard enough. (There was once a nurse in the Cardiac Care Unit of a hospital who gave one of her patients oxygen, whereupon he turned blue and died. Upon investigation, it was learned that the manufacturer had mistakenly put carbon dioxide in a tank marked "oxygen." The nurse was sincere in her belief that oxygen would be breathed by her patient, but she was sincerely wrong. The essential thing was not the sincerity of her faith, but the reliability or unreliability of the object in which she trusted.) We believe that Jesus Christ is Truth, not because of the power or sincerity of our faith, but because He has proven His reliability by His life, death and resurrection.

7. Grow in your own faith:

   a. Study the Scriptures (see 2 Timothy 2:14, 15; 3:14-17). Be sure to evaluate all teaching and new ideas on the basis of the Scriptures and not merely on whether they work.

   b. Be the Church where Christ is known and made known. His teaching is not esoteric and confusing, but simple and practical. Love and serve the world; be broken and distributed like the Bread of Life.

   c. Recognize the element of spiritual warfare (Ephesians 6:10-18; Colossians 1:13-17; 2:13-15; 2 Corinthians 10:3-4). Learn to bind the forces of darkness through prayer and the matchless name of Jesus Christ. Do not attempt ministry in this arena without the protection of the armor of God.

8. Challenge them to investigate the New Testament presentation of Jesus Christ.

When on a flight from Los Angeles to Sydney, I sat next to a young woman who was returning home to Australia from a trip around the world. She had been teaching meditation techniques in different cultural settings. After asking her many questions about her understanding of meditation and spirituality, I asked her what she thought of Jesus Christ. She admitted that although she had been raised in an Anglican religious setting, she did not know very much about Him. She also admitted that she had never read the Bible and, therefore, her view of Jesus had been shaped more by Shirley MacLaine and Elizabeth Clare Prophet than by the New Testament. We began to read about Jesus in the Gospel of John and she was amazed. I shared about my own personal relationship to Christ and challenged her to take my New Testament and investigate for herself the claims of Christ on her life.[7]

Try to correct misconceptions that often exist about what the Bible teaches, and that many New Age people believe merely because someone said it. An example is a statement made in MacLaine's book, *Out on a Limb*:

> The theory of reincarnation is recorded in the Bible. But the proper interpretations were struck from it during an Ecumenical Council meeting of the Catholic Church in Constantinople sometime around 553 A.D., called the Council of Nicea. The Council members voted to strike those teachings from

the Bible in order to solidify Church control.[8]

Her argument went on to say that the early church clergy wanted to get rid of Jesus' teaching on reincarnation in order to keep their authority over the masses. For, if the laity believed in reincarnation and karma, they wouldn't need the salvation being taught by the Church. Yet here is what really happened:

There was such a council at Constantinople in A.D. 553, although it was not called the Council of Nicea. That was a separate event that convened in A.D. 324 and reaffirmed the Church's belief in the deity of Jesus Christ, against the threat of Arianism.

It was not Christ's teaching on reincarnation that was under consideration at Constantinople, but the teaching of Origen (an early Christian theologian) on the preexistence of the soul. This teaching was condemned as heresy. In fact, Judeo-Christian tradition has *never* held to reincarnation. (For more examples of Scripture twisting by New Age advocates, see the Appendix to Chapter 7.)

9. Share your faith in love and with patience.

The following is a testimony from one who became a Christian out of the N.A.M.:

Beneath the crystals, astral trips, and channeled entities are people who are starving for the embrace of Jesus as he says, 'I love you and accept you.' However, since Jesus ascended into heaven and sent his Holy Spirit upon the Church, we as the Church must go in Christ's name and in his love embracing people and calling them out of their sin and into new life in him...When I became a Christian, it was not logic and reason which won me to Christ, although they had their place. It was the love of Jesus Christ that I felt through the lives of caring Christians which brought me to the Father...If...people do not sense our love and commitment to them as people whom Jesus Christ died for, we will make no real, effective penetration into our post-Christian culture...Jesus Christ was able to embrace me because these Christians freely gave of themselves...This authentic New Testament Christianity was totally different from the nonpersonal mysticism I had been practicing...Long hours of theological discussion did not win me to Christ. Love did. Love was the one thing I did not experience in all my New Age journeys and the only thing I was really looking for.[9]

God did not call us to be self-righteous and smug; neither did He call us to be flinching or fearful of those in the N.A.M. Many of them have never seen biblical Christianity in the flesh, nor have they heard of people whose lives were transformed by the gospel. Let us not try to win arguments. Instead let us be sensitive to the spiritual search that is taking many in the N.A.M. down the road of enlightenment and freedom to the destination of spiritual blindness and bondage. Let us minister to them in the power of the Holy Spirit, with all humility and wisdom. Let us be sure that we "preach Christ and Him crucified" (see 1 Corinthians 1:23) and not a gospel based on merely the "felt-needs" of our culture.

Questions for Individual Comprehension or Group Discussion

1. What are your personal feelings about people in general who hold New Age beliefs?

2. How do you feel about those family members and friends who are into the N.A.M.?

3. What are some helpful principles that Paul's approach to the Athenians, in Acts 17, can give us?

4. Can you find some examples where Jesus used the indirect method of asking questions to challenge a certain mind-set?

5. Do you know the proper definitions of key biblical terms so when they are misused, you can recognize the misuse?

   sin =

   repentance =

   born again =

   Jesus Christ =

   God =

   conversion =

   Holy Spirit =

salvation =

second coming =

atonement =

meditation =

eternal life =

truth =

6. Do a serious study of the armor of God in Ephesians 6:10-18. What does each piece represent? How do you put them on?

Endnotes

Chapter 1: An Overview of the *New Age Movement* (N.A.M.)

1. Jose Arngelles, *The Mayan Factor: Path Beyond Technology*, quoted in Jean Callahan, "Cosmic Expectations," *New Age Journal* (Nov.-Dec. 1987) p. 82.

2. Quoted in Ron Enroth, *Lure of the Cults*, (InterVarsity Press, 1988) p. 40.

3. Eldon G. Ernst, "Dimensions of New Religions in American History," Needleman and Baker, eds., *Understanding the New Religions*, (Harper, 1984) p. 44.

4. Enroth, *Lure of the Cults*, p. 42.

5. Marilyn Ferguson, *The Aquarian Conspiracy: Personal and Social Transformation in Our Time*, (J.P. Tarcher, 1980) p. 23.

6. For an excellent presentation of the conspiracy theory, see Chapter 16 of Gary DeMar and Peter Leithart, *The Reduction of Christianity*, (copublished by Dominican Press [Forth Worth] and American Vision Press [Atlanta], 1988).

7. *Time*, (December 7, 1979).

8. Ravi Dykema, "The Mythical Monkey Miracle," *Nexus*, (Fall 1986) p. 4. It proposes a theory based upon a 1953 study of a colony of monkeys on the Japanese island of Koshima. The scenario states that sweet potatoes were given to the monkeys to attract them for observation. One female monkey began washing the dirt off the potatoes before she ate them. Soon, other monkeys began to do the same. Why? The theory proposes that after a "critical mass" was reached—one hundred monkeys who had copied this behavior— all the monkeys on the island began to wash their potatoes before eating. This behavior spread "paranormally" to monkeys on the other islands in the chain.

9. Brooks Alexander, "The Rise of Cosmic Humanism: What is Religion?" *SCP Journal*, 5:1 (1981-82) pp. 1-6.

10. Jeffrey Burton Russell, *Witchcraft In The Middle Ages*, (Cornell Univ. Press, 1972) p. 5.

11. John Eidsmore, *Basic Principles of New Age Thought*, (New Leaf Press, 1991) p. 18.

12. Russell, *Witchcraft In The Middle Ages*, pp. 6-7. Also see Dan Korem, *Streetwise Parents, Foolproof kids*, (Nav Press, 1992) especially Chapter 6.

Chapter 2: New Forms for an Old Lie

1. *Time*, (December 7, 1987). Also see *Enhancing Human Performance: Issues, Theories and Techniques*, by the National Research Council, (National Academy Press, 1988). This paperback book provides incredible information about scientific research done on many New Age techniques used in the field of human performance. Much of the research has been done by the Army in efforts to establish a class of "warrior monk" soldiers. The results proved unfavorable to the New Age cause and, therefore, the Army dropped its paranormal experimentation.

2. Marilyn Ferguson, *The Aquarian Conspiracy*, p. 236.

3. Doug Groothuis, *Unmasking the New Age*, (InterVarsity Press, 1986) p. 123. Also see Ron McRae, "Psychic Warriors," *Omni*, (April 1984) p. 60; Jim Channon, *Evolutionary Tactics*, (privately printed, 1982).

4. Robert Lindsey, "New Age Invades American Way of Life," *International Herald Tribune*, (October 3, 1986).

5. For more information on watchdogging public education for New Age influence, etc., contact Citizens for Excellence in Education, Box 3200, Costa Mesa, CA 92628; 714-546-5931. Also, for questions relating to religious issues in public education, call the Rutherford Institute, 1-800-441-FIRE.

6. Russell Chandler, *Understanding the New Age*, (Word Publishing, 1988) p. 133.

7. Dale Polloch, *Skywalking: The Life and Films of George Lucas*, (Hammay Books, 1983) p. 139.

8. Johanna Michaelsen, *Like Lambs to the Slaughter*, (Harvest House, 1988) p. 233.

9. Billy Bowles, "A Deadly Game?" *Detroit Free Press*, (October 13, 1985).

10. Johanna Michaelsen, *Like Lambs*, p. 62. (See also her discussion of the history of the Ouija, pp. 59-70.)

11. Jane Sterrett, "EST, Get Dressed For Success," *Venture*, (March 1987) p. 53.

12. *Ibid.*, p. 54.

13. *Ibid.*

14. Barbara Blattner, *Holistic Nursing*, (Prentice Hall, 1981) p. 55.

15. Ibid., p. 245.

16. A good overview of this topic can be found in *Spiritual Counterfeits Newsletter*, 14:3, (1989); also, the Spring 1989 issue of the *Journal of Christian Nursing*.

17. Stuart Chevre, "Visualization, Guided Imagery, and the Holistic Health Movement," *S.C.P. Journal*, 9:3 (1990) pp. 21-27.

18. Dr. Terry A. Rondberg, publisher of the "World Chiropractic Alliance," quoted in a *Los*

Angeles Times article that was published in *Daily Hampshire Gazette*, (April 21, 1992).

19. Marcia Greene, "Acupuncture," *SCP Newsletter*, 10:2 (1984) p. 9.

20. For a brief overview of how Gaia is at the root of a developing woman-centered worldview called "Ecofeminism," see the article by Alison Lentini, "The Goddess Comes of Age," *SCP Journal*, 16:1 (1991) pp. 18-22.

21. Tal Brooke, "Gaia—A Religion of the Earth," *SCP Journal*, 16:1 (1991) p. 5.

22. Ross Evans West, "Gaia—She's Alive: A Conversation with James Lovelock," *Orion Nature Quarterly*, 8:1 (1989) p. 58.

23. Deborah Duda, *Coming Home: A Guide to Dying at Home With Dignity*, (Aurora Press, 1987).

24. See appendix to Chapter 6 for an example of how the N.A.M. has influenced the field of counselling.

25. Statistics were quoted from Michaelsen, *Like Lambs*, p. 11.

26. *Ibid.*, p. 85.

27. Chandler, *Understanding the New Age*, p. 81.

28. F. LaGard Smith, *Out on a Broken Limb*, (Harvest House, 1989) p. 102.

29. Dan Korem, in his fascinating book, *Powers: Testing the Psychic and Supernatural*, (InterVarsity Press, 1988), claims that in his career as an investigative reporter, he has not seen

one substantiated case of genuine psychic power. He believes that all forms of psychic phenomena are deceptions and that we must learn how to discern satan's lies.

30. Tell your children some of the following:

a. God is the Creator of Heaven and Earth.

b. Man has dominion over the Earth, not the other way around.

c. God is God; not the Earth, not a man.

d. Man has polluted the Earth; he has not been a good steward.

e. Christians believe in preserving our environment and ecosystems.

f. Christians reject "Mother Earth" as God.

g. Christians do not believe in oneness with the Earth; the Earth serves man's needs, and man should be its gardener.

h. People are more important to God than animals and the Earth.

An excellent book for this purpose is *Under the spell of MOTHER EARTH* by Berit Kjos, (Victor Books: Scripture Press, 1992).

Chapter 3:   Historical Roots and Causative Factors of the New Age Movement

1. This brief history was taken from Dean Halverson, "A History and Analysis of the New

Thought Movement," *SCP Journal*, 11:1 (1985) pp. 1, 5-10.

2. Horatio Dresser, "A History of the New Thought Movement," p. 211, as quoted in Halverson, "A History and Analysis," p. 10.

3. The Unity School of Christianity publishes the following periodicals, which you may even have in your home: *Unity, Daily Word, Wee Wisdom*.

4. J. Weldon and P. Carden, "Ernest Holmes and Religious Science," *Forward*, 7:1 pp. 7, 16-19.

5. Dave Hunt, *The Seduction of Christianity*, (Harvest House, 1986) p. 25.

6. F.C.S. Schiller, "Spiritualism," James Hastings, ed., *Encyclopedia of Religion and Ethics*, XI, (Scribner, 1921) p. 807.

7. "A Matter of Course: Conversation With Kenneth Wapnick," an interview by Dean Halverson, *SCP Journal*, 7:1 (1987) pp. 8-17.

8. In 1907, *The Aquarian Gospel of Jesus the Christ* was published by Levi H. Dowling, alias Levi, who claimed to have received the material in a vision and transcribed it in just a few hours. It allegedly contains a record of 18 of the "lost years" of Jesus in which He supposedly travelled to Tibet, India, Russia and Greece.

9. More information on the "I AM" Movement can be found in Walter Martin's book, *The New Cults*, (Vision House, 1978), especially Ch. 6, pp. 204-234.

10. Stephen Hoeller, "The Gnostic Jung," *Quest,* (Summer 1989) p. 86.

11. See Fromm's *The Dogma of Christ and Other Essays,* (Holt, Rinehart and Winston, 1955); and *You Shall Be As Gods,* (Holt, Rinehart and Winston, 1966).

12. Paul C. Vitz, *Psychology As Religion: The Cult of Self Worship,* (Eerdmans, 1977) p. 20.

13. See A. Maslow, *The Farther Reaches of Human Nature,* (Penguin, 1979).

14. Carl R. Rogers, *Counselling and Psychotherapy,* (Houghton Mifflin, 1942) p. 244.

15. Carl R. Rogers, *On Becoming a Person,* (Houghton Mifflin, 1961) p. 8.

16. Fred A. Wolf, *Taking the Quantum Leap: The New Physics for Non-Scientists,* (Harper and Row, 1989) p. 63.

17. Fritsof Capra, *The Tao of Physics,* (Shambhala, 1975) p. 25.

18. Wolf, *Taking the Quantum Leap,* p. 183.

19. *Ibid.,* p. 6.

20. Groothuis, *Unmasking the New Age,* p. 104.

21. Richard H. Bube, "Science and Pseudo-Science," *The Reformed Journal,* (November 1982) p. 11. Also see Stanley Jaki, *The Road of Science and the Ways to God,* (University of Chicago Press, 1980).

22. "The New Age of Aquarius," *Newsweek*, (February 3, 1992) pp. 65-67.

23. J. Gordon Melton, "How New Is New? The Flowering of the 'New' Religious Consciousness since 1965," David G. Bromley and Philip E. Hammond, eds., *The Future of New Religious Movements*, (Mercer University Press, 1987) pp. 48-51.

24. *Ibid.*, p. 51.

25. Marilyn Ferguson, *The Aquarian Conspiracy*, p. 434. The people most often named, in order of frequency, were Pierre Teilhard de Chardin, C.G. Jung, Abraham Maslow, Carl Rogers, Aldous Huxley, Roberto Assagioli and J. Krishnamurti.

26. Many of these groups are evaluated from a Christian perspective in: Walter Martin, *The New Cults*, (Vision House, 1978); Ron Enroth et al., *A Guide to Cults and New Religions*, (InterVarsity Press, 1983).

27. Marcia Greene, "A Christian Consideration of Human Potential," *SCP Journal*, 5:1 (1981-1982) p. 34.

28. Marilyn Ferguson, *The Aquarian Conspiracy*, pp. 25-26, 32.

29. Russell Chandler, *Understanding The New Age*, (Word Publishing, 1988) p. 51.

Chapter 4: Worldviews

1. For more study on comparative worldviews, consider the following: James Sire, *The Universe Next Door*, (InterVarsity Press, 1988); Norman

Geisler and William Watkins, *Worlds Apart: A Handbook on Worldviews,* (Baker Book House, 1989); William Hasker, *Metaphysics: Constructing a World View,* (InterVarsity Press, 1983); Brooks Alexander and Robert Burrows, "New Age and Biblical World Views," *SCP Newsletter,* 10:5 (1984-1985) pp. 18-20.

2. Quoted in Douglas Groothuis, *Unmasking the New Age,* (InterVarsity Press, 1986) p. 21.

3. Meditations of Maharishi Mahesh Yogi, (Bantam Books, 1968) p. 178.

4. Shirley MacLaine, *Dancing in the Light,* (Bantam Books, 1985) p. 420.

5. *What's So* (magazine of the *EST* movement), (October 1974).

6. There is an indication within Eastern religious thought that "some things are more one than others"—that some things appear to be closer to the "One" than others do. The hierarchy proceeds from mineral, vegetable, animal to human. Some of humanity is closer to the "One" than others are.

7. Christmas Humphreys, *Buddhism,* 3rd edition, (Penguin, 1962) p. 203.

8. Brooks Alexander, "Visualizing the Tower of Babel," *SCP Journal,* 9:3 (1990) p. 7.

9. Kenneth Walker, *I Saw Hitler Make Black Magic,* (The Prosperos [Santa Monica], 1948).

Chapter 5:   Evaluation of the New Age Movement: Points of Agreement

1. See the article by R.C. Sproul, "The Origin of the Soul," *Tabletalk*, (June 1992) pp. 4-7.

2. Kathryn Baker, "Creativity and the God of Life," *SCP Newsletter*, 11:3 (1985) p. 6.

3. Christians disagree as to the nature of this impact. There are three main views, which can be illustrated by the following analogies: 1) Christians are guests in an old house (which represents the world) that is starting to cave in. They rush to hold up the ceiling and the walls so some of the occupants have time to get out to safety before everything goes; 2) Christians are the remodeling company that is trying to rebuild the very structure of the dilapidated house; and 3) Christians are a construction company that has given up on the old house and has started to build a new one next door.

4. Jeremy Rifkin, *The Emerging Order: God in the Age of Scarcity*, (Putnam and Sons, 1979).

5. Marcia Green, "Acupuncture," *SCP Newsletter*, 10:2 (1984) p. 9.

6. An excellent book on New Age medical practices is: Reisser, Reisser, Weldon, *New Age Medicine*, (InterVarsity Press, 1987).

Chapter 6:   Evaluation of the New Age Movement: Points of Disagreement

1. C.S. Lewis, *The Problem of Pain*, (Macmillan Co., 1962) pp. 150-151.

2. Elizabeth Clare Prophet, a taped lecture given in Los Angeles at the Conference on Spiritual Freedom, 1990.

3. John White, "Jesus and the Idea of a New Age," *The Quest,* (Summer 1989) pp. 13-23.

4. Helen Wambach, a taped lecture given in Palo Alto, California July 15, 1979.

5. Shirley MacLane, *Dancing in the Light,* (Bantam Books, 1985) p. 360.

6. Shirley MacLaine, *Out on a Limb,* (Bantam Books, 1987) p. 201.

7. Ibid., p. 199.

8. Martin Gardner, "Issness Is Her Business," *N.Y. Review,* (April 9, 1987) p. 18.

9. It should be noted that there are legitimate uses of imagination: an artist "sees" her finished work before she begins; the athlete mentally prepares for the game by "rehearsing" it in his mind; the architect "visualizes" her project; the storyteller creates "images" in the minds of his hearers. These are distinguished from creating or controlling reality through mind-power.

Chapter 7:   Hints on Relating to Those in the N.A.M.

1. John White, *Jesus and the Idea of a New Age,* pp. 13-23.

2. H. Reiker, *The Yoga of Light,* (Dawn House, 1974) p. 9.

3. Weldon and Wilson, *Occult Shock and Psychic Forces*, (Master Books, 1980) pp. 7-9.

4. Christina and Stanislov Grut, *Spiritual Emergency: The Understanding and Treatment of Transpersonal Crisis*, (Pyramid Books, 1987).

5. Yoga Journal, (July/August 1986) p. 40. Also note S. Hunt, *Ouija, The Most Dangerous Game*, (Pyramid Books, 1991).

6. The Associated Press, May 3, 1988.

7. An excellent resource for presenting Christ to a New Ager is found in Doug Groothuis, *Revealing the New Age Jesus*, (InterVarsity Press, 1990); especially Chapter 3, "Claims and Credentials of Christ."

8. Shirley MacLaine, *Out on a Limb*, pp. 234-5.

9. Paul McGuire, *Evangelizing the New Age*, (Servant Publications, 1989) pp. 89-90.

Appendix to Chapter 6

On Visualization and Christianity

It is crucial that we understand the issue of visualization because it is in this area that many Christians open themselves up to a New Age influence. There needs to be a sharp distinction made between biblical spirituality, with its emphasis on faith and submission to the will of God, and humanistic spirituality, which emphasizes the techniques of controlling events and circumstances. A.W. Tozer said the following about visualization: "We must distinguish believing from visualizing. The two are not the same. One is moral and the other is mental...the ability to visualize is found among vigorous-minded persons, whatever their moral or spiritual condition may be...The wise Christian will not let his assurance depend on his powers of imagination" (*That Incredible Christian*, Harrisburg, PA: Christian Publication, 1964).

Tozer's counsel is a wise one, especially since some Christians are practicing methods of visualization in order to deepen their relationship to God and to become more effective in prayer. Richard Foster, for example, in his 1978 edition of *Celebration of Discipline*, included a very controversial section containing a visualization exercise of ascending into Heaven. "In your imagination allow your spiritual body, shining with light, to rise out of your physical body. Look back...and reassure your body that you will return momentarily. Imagine your spiritual self, alive and vibrant, rising up through the clouds and into the stratosphere...Go deeper and deeper into outer space until there is nothing except the warm presence of the eternal Creator" (p. 27). Anyone familiar with classic Shamanism recognizes out-of-body experiences and ascents or flights into deeper space as a part of its spiritual system, not that of Christianity.

The same concern arises when one listens to Norman Vincent Peale admit that mind-power is an independent, humanly controllable force that can "act at a distance" (*Positive Imaging*, Old Tappan, NJ: Fleming Revell/Spire, 1982). Also, there is concern when one hears Paul Yongii Cho promote visualization as a form of prayer: "If you cannot visualize clearly in your heart exactly what you hope for, it cannot become a reality to you" (*The Fourth Dimension*, Plainfield, NJ: Logos, 1979).

How am I to evaluate these techniques and concepts that are being offered by respectable men to help me in my spiritual journey? I must first ask, "What does Scripture say?" With so many voices, I need guidance. I see little, if any, biblical evidence for the spiritual technique of visualization. Instead, I read of men and women on their knees before God petitioning, not manipulating; seeking God's will, not imposing their own; believing, not visualizing. If they did have a vision or an extraordinary spiritual experience it was not because they sought it, but because it was given to them by a sovereign God.

The second question I must ask is, "What, if any, is the legitimate use of imagination in my spiritual exercises?" Let me quote some very wise counsel by Brooks Alexander in his article in *SCP Journal* (9:3, 1990, p. 20):

There is nothing wrong with inner imagery *per se*. Our imagination is a gift of God, and it was given to be used. But here is a simple rule of thumb for exercising that gift in religious and spiritual life. Use images in prayer as a means of communicating *to* God. Do not use your own created images as a source of communication *from* God. Do not use images as instruments of control, having power in themselves because of their nature...When we use our imagination to speak to God or to make Biblical history vivid, we are doing what is natural and intended...When we use our fallen imagination to hear *from* God, or to manipulate reality, we are treading in the shadows between Shamanism and superstition!

* * * * * *

I recently attended a seminar for health care workers that was sponsored by the Department of Psychiatry at a local hospital. The presenter was a licensed social worker in private practice, and the seminar was entitled, *Imagery and Visualization: Honoring the Language of the Internal World.* The basis of her presentation was called "The Personal Totem Pole Process," developed by Eligio Stephen Gollegos, which "provides a direct route to our internal world and its language, which is imagery."

She admitted that such was a decidedly non-Western approach to therapy. She used the following terms during her discourse to describe this method: "right-brain," "women's-way-of-knowing," "non-linear," "non-logic," "pre-verbal," "symbolic" and "creative." Upon questioning, she denied that this method had anything to do with Eastern religious spirituality. She said it was basically "physical" and was just another way of doing psychotherapy. She explained the existence of "autonomous imagery" as a being or object that we meet within ourselves through meditation and which should not be questioned rationally.

Then she took those in attendance on a thirty-minute, guided imagery tour of their internal world. She used basic yoga techniques of breathing and relaxation. She then asked participants to "center" or concentrate on the area of their solar plexus ("third chakra") and imagine meeting an object, person or animal there. They were to ask this object if it had anything to teach them. Then, they were to say to the object, "Is there something I can do for you?" We were told that we should listen and do whatever it said, if we were willing. Our seminar leader's therapeutic principle was that we should "respectfully accept whatever that autonomous image is and says" without question.

Interestingly, one woman behind me related that the image that appeared to her was that of a snake, coiled and red. It spoke to her, claimed to be her friend and began to tell her secrets about her ex-husband. She was visibly shaken.

I prayed fervently during the imagery session for spiritual protection over all those in the room, especially those who were Christians. I made a public statement that visualization techniques were derived from an occult-based spirituality and that no amount of scientific-sounding vocabulary was likely to make it a legitimate psychotherapeutic technique. I also spoke to the therapist afterwards and warned her of the dangers of the demonic and of transpersonal emergencies. (A transpersonal emergency occurs when a person experiences shock or some other form of crisis while in a meditative state. An increasing volume of material is being written on this phenomenon.) I

was accused of being intolerant of a therapy that
has growing acceptance by those in the medical
and scientific world.

Appendix to Chapter 7

The Abused Bible

The Bible is often used by those in the N.A.M. to show that their belief system is compatible with Christianity. Unfortunately, these attempts are abuses of the text—twisting of words or phrases beyond their original meaning in the context.

The following are examples of how specific passages in the Bible have been used (abused) to support some of the major teachings of the N.A.M. I will attempt to present a proper interpretation of each passage based upon its context. (I would direct the reader to a fuller account of such passages in the book, *Scripture Twisting: 20 Ways the Cults Misread the Bible* [Downers Grove: Inter-Varsity Press, 1980] by James Sire. Although it does not specifically deal with the N.A.M., his handy reference guide to these twenty errors of interpretation is excellent [pp. 155-160].)

Humanity Is God

John 10:34

Jesus answered them, "Has it not been written in your Law, 'I said, you are gods'?"

This passage is often used as evidence that Jesus taught the divinity of our humanity. Is this really a proper interpretation? I believe that a look at the context of this passage will indicate a different conclusion.

Jesus was engaged in deep controversy with the Jewish leaders of His day. He had just claimed that "I and the Father are one" (v. 30). It is obvious, both from the reaction of the Jews as well as from the subsequent comments of Jesus, that He had made the claim to be God (of *one* substance with the Father). It was in the face of this indictment of blasphemy that Jesus responded with the verse under consideration. He was actually quoting Psalm 82:6,7: "I said, 'You are gods, and all of you are sons of the Most High. Nevertheless you will die like men, and fall like any one of the princes.' " This Psalm pictures God speaking to the judges of Israel and condemning them for their injustice. These judges were called "gods" because they made decisions on behalf of God. The context clearly shows that these judges were mere mortals and not really divine beings.

Jesus took the thought of this Psalm and used it to defend His claim to be God. He acknowledged that not one of these religious leaders had ever condemned the Scriptures because it called these mortal judges "gods." Why then should they condemn Him who truly was the unique Son of God?

2 Peter 1:4

> *For by these He has granted to us His precious and magnificent promises, in order that by them you might become partakers of the divine nature, having escaped the corruption that is in the world by lust.*

This verse is sometimes used by New Age adherents to show that the Bible supports the idea that we discover our divinity by escaping this physical world of unreality. Can this belief really be supported, as we examine the context?

Peter is writing to those who had received Jesus Christ as Savior. He goes on to teach that having such a relationship to Christ produces certain qualities in one's life. It produces grace and peace, as well as the power to live a holy life. The source of this power is the divine nature that Christians receive when they believe in Christ. This power for holy living enables them to escape seduction by a society in rebellion against God.

This text says exactly the opposite of what the N.A.M. wants it to say. It does not indicate that we discover our "deified self" by escaping the physical world through yoga or other meditative techniques. However, it does say that as we enter into a faith-union with Jesus Christ, His indwelling nature enables us to escape the very real corruption of a very real world.

Reincarnation

John 3:3

> *Jesus answered and said to him, "Truly, truly, I say to you, unless one is born again, he cannot see the kingdom of God."*

This verse has been used many times by the N.A.M. to claim that Jesus actually taught reincarnation. The term "born again" is used interchangeably with the term "reborn again." James Sire calls this a case of *confused definitions* where an ordinary biblical term is redefined within a completely different system of thought. (See Chapter 7, point 3, for a list of biblical terms and their redefinitions.)

The context of this verse is Jesus' conversation with Nicodemus, a Jewish religious leader who sought a private audience with this young Rabbi. When Jesus told him that he must be born again in order to perceive the things of God, Nicodemus showed a complete misunderstanding of what was said. He thought Jesus was saying that he must enter a second time into his mother's womb and be born again. Literally, the term that Jesus used is best translated as either "born anew" or "born from above." Therefore, the man who would enter into the Kingdom of God must be born in a fundamentally new fashion. His rebirth must not be the result of human action, but of the Holy Spirit's. It must not be from earth, but from Heaven. It must not be merely a repetition of the old, but something radically new. This is the force of Jesus' clarification to Nicodemus: "Truly, truly, I say to you, unless one is born of water and the Spirit, he cannot enter into the kingdom of God. That which is born of the flesh is flesh; and that which is born of the Spirit is spirit" (vv. 5,6).

I think it significant that the New Age misunderstanding of this text parallels that of Nicodemus. Both have interpreted the term "born again" to mean a physical rebirth. Those in the N.A.M. should strive to understand Jesus' meaning within the text instead of substituting their own. Perhaps they, like Nicodemus, would then become followers of Jesus Christ.

Jeremiah 1:5

> *Before I formed you in the womb I knew you, and before you were born I consecrated you; I have appointed you a prophet to the nations.*

This text has been "used" not only by the N.A.M. to support reincarnation, but also by the Mormons to document their belief in the preexistence of the soul. (This belief claims that we all existed as spirit beings in Heaven before we occupied our bodies.)

The context of this passage is the call of Jeremiah to his prophetic office. The language is of an all-knowing God giving the young prophet a glimpse of how thorough His knowledge is concerning Jeremiah's life. There is not one word about reincarnation, nor about the preexistence of Jeremiah's soul. We are told only that God created Jeremiah in his mother's womb and that He chose him to be a prophet while he was still a fetus. I think pro-life advocates have more in this verse to substantiate their position than do the Mormons and the N.A.M.

Questioning the Authority of the Bible

John 5:39

> *You search the Scriptures, because you think that in them you have eternal life...*

There are some New Age thinkers who have lifted these words of Jesus right out of their context to show that Christians place too much emphasis on the Bible. This is an amazing case of abusing the text and making it say the opposite of what it means.

If these interpreters would only finish the statement in the passage, they would see their faulty conclusion. "...and it is these that bear witness of Me; and you are unwilling to come to Me, that you may have life" (vv. 39-40). This passage is an accusation by Jesus that the Jewish religious leaders were giving too little attention to the Scriptures rather than too much. For, if they really studied the Old Testament, they would see that it spoke of Jesus and how He alone could give them eternal life. The New Age interpretation once again implodes.

Matthew 5:21,22

> *You have heard that the ancients were told,*
> *"You shall not commit murder" and*
> *"Whoever commits murder shall be liable*
> *to the court." But I say to you that every one*
> *who is angry with his brother shall be guilty*
> *before the court; and whoever shall say to*
> *his brother, "Raca," shall be guilty before*
> *the supreme court; and whoever shall say,*
> *"You fool," shall be guilty enough to go into*
> *the* [fiery] *hell...*

This passage, as well as the five other texts of similar structure in this chapter, is cited by the N.A.M. to prove that Jesus contradicted the Scriptures with His "But I say to you." A careful reading of each passage will indicate that, once again, the opposite is true.

Jesus had just finished saying, "Do not think that I came to abolish the Law or the Prophets; I did not come to abolish, but to fulfill" (v. 17). Therefore, what Jesus did in these subsequent passages must have something to do with His fulfillment of the Scriptures. He was saying that there is more to the Law than an external command. He expanded the understanding of the Law to include an inner or spiritual requirement. The sixth commandment, for example, is fulfilled by not harboring hatred in the heart as well as by not doing physical violence to another person.

These texts indicate that Jesus not only had high regard for the commandments but also sought to amplify their meaning to include one's thoughts and motives as well as one's behavior.

A Wild One

I cannot close this section without bringing to your attention an incredible interpretation that was made by a very respected New Age author, which was found in a very credible New Age journal.

Matthew 11:29,30

> *Take My yoke upon you, and learn from Me, for I am gentle and humble in heart; and you shall find rest for your souls. For My yoke is easy, and My load is light.*

This New Age author interprets the passage as an example of Jesus' teaching His disciples about the use of various spiritual exercises. Let me quote directly from this article.

The word "yoke" is conventionally understood to mean "burden" or "work." However, it is better understood in the sense of the Sanskrit *yug*, meaning "to yoke or join." It is the root from which "yoga" comes, and yoga is a system of spiritual practices designed to accelerate spiritual growth and development... so that the yogi attains union with the Divine. That yoking was precisely the aim of Jesus' teaching. Thus esoteric Christianity understands the verses to mean "the practices I prescribe for growth to Christ consciousness" (John White, "Jesus and the Idea

of a New Age," *The Quest*, Summer 1989,
p. 20).

We see not only a complete disregard for the
context of this verse, but also a disregard for the
meaning of the words that Jesus used and His disciples understood. With one wave of his interpre-
tive wand, the author changes Jesus from a Jewish
rabbi into a Hindu holy man.

* * * * * *

If nothing else, this section will have taught you
the importance of interpreting a biblical text by its
context. The second truth you will have learned is
that most New Age interpretations of the Bible are
"privitistic." In other words, the interpreter is the
final authority on the text and feels no obligation
to have his conclusions substantiated either by
logic or by the wider community, for they have
come from within himself.

A case in point concerns the "sleeping prophet,"
Edgar Cayce, who claimed to accept the Bible as
God's Word. Yet he subjected his understanding of
the Bible to his psychic experiences, rather than
measure his experiences by the Scriptures. Thus,
he moved away from his once orthodox faith: "In
1923, Cayce awoke from a trance in Dayton, Ohio,
to be told that he had asserted the reality of reincarnation. At that time Cayce did not himself
believe in reincarnation; but when his sleeping self
had repeatedly affirmed its reality, he came to
terms with it, and incorporated it into his orthodox

Christian doctrine" (Colin Wilson, *The Occult: A History*, Random House, 1971, p. 168).

As Christians, we believe that the Bible is our final authority, one not subject to our private interpretation or experience. Article Two of the Lausanne Covenant (1974) says, "We affirm the divine inspiration, truthfulness and authority of both the Old and New Testament Scriptures in their entirety as the only written Word of God, without error in all that it affirms, and the only infallible rule of faith and practice." Therefore, Evangelicals assert that any experience, interpretation, doctrine or movement must be measured by the yardstick of the Scriptures.

2 Corinthians 4:1-6 (NIV)

Therefore, since through God's mercy we have [received] *this ministry* [of sharing the gospel], *we do not lose heart. Rather, we have renounced secret and* [sinful] *ways; we do not use deception, nor do we distort the word of God. On the contrary, by setting forth the truth plainly we commend ourselves to every man's conscience in the sight of God. And even if our gospel is veiled, it is veiled to those who are perishing. The god of this age has blinded the minds of unbelievers, so that they cannot see the light of the gospel of the glory of Christ, who is the image of God. For we do not preach ourselves, but Jesus Christ as Lord, and ourselves as your servants for Jesus' sake. For God who said, "Let light shine out of darkness," made His light* [to] *shine in our hearts to give us the light of the knowledge of the glory of God in the face of Christ.*

Glossary of Terms
(Taken from a variety of sources.)

ACUPUNCTURE. An HOLISTIC health technique that defines disease as an imbalance in "energy flow"; seeks to restore and redirect the flow and balance by inserting needles at key points in the body. Acupuncture, acupressure and allied therapies are derived from ancient Chinese medicine and philosophy.

ANGEL CARDS. A series of matchbook-size cards, each with a picture of an angel and the name of a positive virtue, such as "strength," "joy," "integrity," "enthusiasm." Each day a card is to be chosen, meditated upon and visualized so the angel can become one with the seeker and the energy of the virtue experienced.

APPORT. A phenomenon often associated with seances, whereby an object is said to be dissolved into an invisible form and then carried by energy to another location and there materialized. Madame Helena Blavatsky claimed to have materialized, at a seance, the belt buckle buried with her father's body in Russia.

ASCENDED MASTERS. Spiritual leaders from past times who have died and become one with "God"; who are then appointed from the spiritual world to communicate "truth" to those still living through the practice of CHANNELING.

ASTRAL. A non-physical level of consciousness characterized primarily by emotion. Said to be the place where most humans go after they die and where they exist between earthly incarnations. An astral projection, or Out-of-Body Experience (OBE), is an experience where one seems to be in a place separate from one's physical body while fully and normally conscious. The experience, which may be hallucinatory in nature, can be spontaneous or induced. The astral and physical bodies generally remain connected by a distended "cord" during the projection.

ASTROLOGY. The OCCULT art or "religious science" that deciphers the influence that cosmic forces radiating from celestial bodies supposedly have on earth, particularly upon humankind. Astrology originated at least 5,000 years ago, probably in Babylon. It was based on the erroneous belief that the earth is the center of the universe and is circled by the ZODIAC (planets).

AURA. An apparent envelope or field of colored radiation said to surround the human body and other animate objects, with the color or colors indicating different aspects of the person's physical, psychological and spiritual condition. (See also KIRLIAN.)

AUTOMATIC WRITING. Writing done without conscious muscular effort; i.e., not under the conscious control of the writer.

BIOFEEDBACK. A technique using instruments to self-monitor what are normally unconscious, involuntary body processes such as brain waves, heartbeat and muscle tension. As this information is fed back to the person, it is believed that he or she can then learn to consciously and voluntarily control internal biological functions.

BOJI STONES. Small, black, metallic-like stones allegedly from the base of a mysterious pyramid somewhere in the U.S. and purified by means of ASTRAL light. It is to be worn around the neck to keep the body's energy field in balance. It is also alleged to have healing qualities, due to the theory that all disease stems from imbalance in the body.

CHANNELING. A process of receiving information from some level of consciousness beyond the "self" as it is generally understood. A "channeler," or medium, usually goes into a TRANCE to establish contact with a spirit, ASCENDED MASTER, higher consciousness or some other entity, and then receives and repeats messages from "the other side" of the physical world.

CHAKRAS. The seven energy points vertically aligned in the human body, according to New Agers and YOGI(S). "Raising" the KUNDALINI or serpent powers up through the chakras is the aim of YOGA meditation. Enlightenment (Samadhi) is achieved when the kundalini reaches the "crown chakra" at the top of the head.

CHIROMANCY. (Known to most as Palm Reading.) A means of predicting important life events by "reading" the lines on a person's hand.

CLAIRAUDIENCE. The mental "hearing" of extra-sensory data.

CLAIRVOYANCE. Mental "seeing" of physical objects or events from a distance by PSYCHIC means. Distinguished from TELEPATHY, which involves ESP.

CONSCIOUSNESS. The state of mental awareness or present "knowing." New Agers usually refer to consciousness as the awareness or perception of one's "inner-self," or of an inward awareness of external objects or facts.

DEEP ECOLOGY. A spiritualized perspective on the environment that emphasizes that humans have no more rights on this earth than other forms of life. The proper ecological view, according to the N.A.M., is to shift our perspective from a human-centered one toward a larger awareness of "life as a whole."

DIVINATION. Methods of discovering the personal, human significance of present or future events. Such methods may include dreams, hunches, involuntary body actions, mediumistic possession, consulting the dead, observing the behavior of animals and birds, tossing coins, casting lots and "reading" TAROT cards and RUNES.

DOWSING. A form of CLAIRVOYANCE in which underground water, minerals or other substances are apparently located by means of a V-shaped or divining rod or stick.

DRUIDISM. From the Gaelic word meaning "a wise man" or "magician." Religion of the ancient Celts, who practiced human/animal sacrifice and foretold future events by watching the death-agony of a victim or by examining its entrails.

ECO-FEMINISM. A feminist ecological perspective that sees environmental problems as the result of "patriarchy," a male-centered view of the earth and its resources. It finds the solution in a woman-centered cosmology based upon a religious belief in the goddess GAIA (also named Diana, Artemis, Delphene, Kali, Ishtar, Ashtoreth, Isis, Coatlique, Yoraba, Mary).

ESOTERIC. Literally means something "inner" or "within." That which is hidden from the public and revealed only to a special group. Related to OCCULT.

ESP. *Extra Sensory Perception*; the experience of, or response to, an external event, object, state or influence without apparent contact through the known senses. ESP may occur without those involved being aware of it.

GAIA. (Pronounced gay-a.) The earth goddess of the ancient Greeks. She is now identified to many New Age groups as Mother Earth, the eternal source of life. (See also ECO-FEMINISM.)

GNOSTICISM. An heretical movement of the second century. The term comes from the Greek word *gnosis*, which means "knowledge." The Gnostics claimed special secret knowledge that could be possessed by a class of humanity called the "pneumatics," or spirituals. All Gnostics taught that matter was evil and that the heavenly Christ took possession of the man Jesus, but never became human. They also taught that the God of the Bible was not the Supreme God, but an inferior being called the Demiurge, who created the material (evil) world.

GUIDED IMAGERY. A process whereby one enters into a meditative state and visualizes a person, animal or object. This entity is then engaged in conversation and asked to give wisdom on healing or self-improvement.

GURU. A spiritual teacher who instructs disciples in the "way" of enlightenment. The guru's authority is to be implicitly accepted.

HATHA-YOGA. One of about ten forms of YOGA; the one most often taught to the general public. *Hatha* means "to suppress." Its purpose is to suppress the flow of psychic energy on either side of the spinal column, thus forcing the KUNDALINI up through the central psychic channel in the spine and up through the CHAKRAS.

HIGHER SELF. The most "spiritual" and "knowing" part of oneself, the God within you. It is said to lie beyond the ego, the day-to-day personality and the personal unconscious. The Higher Self can be channeled for wisdom and guidance. Variations include the Over-Soul, the Superconsciousness, the Atman, the Christ (or Krishna or Buddha) Consciousness.

HOLISTIC. Alternatively, but less frequently, spelled "wholistic"; derived from the Greek *holos*, meaning "whole" in the sense of "entire" or "unified." Holistic health practices emphasize the whole person, the impact of the environment and the interdependence of all parts of the body, mind and spirit in the prevention and treatment of ailments.

HOROSCOPE. The arrangement of the planets and stars at the moment of a person's birth. It is also a forecast of the person's future, based upon such an arrangement.

HYPNOSIS. A state of mind resembling a deep sleep or TRANCE. The person who is hypnotized maintains control of his will and feelings, but acts according to suggestions presented. A heightened state of suggestibility.

I CHING. Chinese book of DIVINATION associated with TAOISM; the ancient system of telling fortunes by throwing sticks or tossing coins to form certain patterns that are said to reveal unconscious tendencies.

IRIDOLOGY. A HOLISTIC health treatment based upon the belief that the eye mirrors the soul and that a study of the iris of the eye can detect disease in the body.

KABALA. A system of Jewish OCCULT MYSTICISM developed by certain rabbis during the Middle Ages that relies heavily on mathematical interpretation of the Scriptures. Also spelled "Cabala."

KARMA. A Hindu term for the "law" of justice, or cause and effect, requiring that the accumulated effect of one's actions in this life determines the type of existence the soul will have in the next life; you reap what you sow. (See also REINCARNATION.)

KIRLIAN. A method of supposedly capturing on a photographic plate an image of the electromagnetic energy (AURA) that emanates from plants, animals and humans.

KUNDALINI. Psycho-spiritual energy thought by YOGI(S) to lie dormant at the base of the spine. Believed to be a snake-like goddess, kundalini is referred to as "the serpent power."

MAGIC (or MAGICK). Any practice or ritual whereby one seeks to control the powers or forces of the universe in a self-serving way. Modern adherents of the craft tend to draw inspiration from the KABALA. The OCCULT practice should not be confused with the sleight-of-hand tricks that we also know as magic.

MANDALA. A word from Sanskrit meaning "circle" or "center." Usually an asymmetrical figure or geometrical pattern used as a focus of concentration in Yoga. Serves a similar purpose of a MANTRA.

MANTRA. A "holy" word, phrase or verse in Hindu or Buddhist meditation techniques (such as OM). A mantra is usually provided to an initiate by a GURU who is supposed to hold specific insights regarding the needs of his pupils. The vibrations of the mantra are said to lead the meditator into union with the divine source within him.

MONISM. Literally means "one." As a spiritual framework, it refers to the classical OCCULT philosophy that "All is One"; all reality may be reduced to a single, unifying principle partaking of the same essence and reality. Monism is also related to PANTHEISM in that there is no ultimate distinction between the Creator and the creation, that "All is God."

MYSTICISM. The belief that God is totally different from anything the human mind can rationally imagine and so must be approached by a mind without content. Spiritual union or direct communion with Ultimate Reality can be obtained only through subjective experiences such as intuition or meditation.

NATURALISM. The worldview of secular humanism: asserts that nothing beyond nature is real. Human beings are, therefore, to be understood strictly in terms of heredity and environment. (Not a New Age or Christian belief system.)

NIRVANA. Literally, a "blowing out" or a "cooling" of the fires of existence. It is the main word used in Buddhism for final release from the cycle of birth and death into bliss. The end-stage of REINCARNATION.

NOSTRADAMUS. A 16th century French OCCULTist whose book *The Centuries* contains numerous poetic prophecies that have become a fashionable form of DIVINATION. His colorful, highly metaphorical and oblique language has been interpreted as predicting certain modern events such as the rise of Hitler and the assassination of President Kennedy.

OCCULT. From the Latin word *occultus,* meaning "concealed." The occult refers to beliefs and practices of the mystic arts, including: MAGIC, alchemy, ASTROLOGY, etc. Closely related to ESOTERIC.

OUIJA BOARD. (Pronounced we-gee.) From the French "oui" and the German "ja," meaning "yes." A wooden board with letters and numerals arranged in crescent shapes, used with a tripod at whose apex is a pointer. When one or more persons place their fingers lightly upon the pointer it spells out "messages" by stopping at letters. Some believe that the pointer is directed either by the unconscious mind or by spirit influence. Others believe that the board game is operated by demons. The board is often used in spiritualistic seances to "relay messages from the dead."

PAGAN (or NEOPAGAN). One who believes in the pre-Christian nature religions of the West: goddess religions, ancient European, tribal religions, etc.

PANTHEISM. Belief that God and the world are ultimately identical; "All is God." Everything that exists constitutes a unity; this all-inclusive unity is divine. God is the forces and laws of the universe, but is not a Being with personality.

PARANORMAL. Phenomena that are studied in PSYCHIC research. They are "beyond the normal" in terms of explanation.

POLTERGEIST. German for "noisy ghost." Supposedly exhibits various PARANORMAL manifestations involving the breaking and movement of objects.

PSI. The twenty-third letter of the Greek alphabet; a general New Age term for ESP, PSYCHOKINESIS, TELEPATHY, CLAIRVOYANCE, CLAIRAUDIENCE, precognition and other PARANORMAL phenomena that are nonphysical in nature.

PSYCHIC. A medium, "sensitive" or channeler. It is also an adjective describing PARANORMAL events that can't be explained by established physical principles.

PSYCHOKINESIS. The power of the mind to influence matter or to move objects. Popularly known as PK. (See also TELEKINESIS.)

PSYCHOMETRY. PARANORMALLY obtaining information about a person, simply through touching or handling a physical object belonging to that person.

REFLEXOLOGY. A HOLISTIC health care practice based upon the belief that the foot is the key to understanding bodily defects. Therefore, massaging certain points on the foot will help align the energy balance of the body.

REINCARNATION. A belief that the soul moves from one bodily existence to another until it is released from historical existence and absorbed into the Absolute. (See also KARMA.)

RUNES. From the Gothic *rana*, which means "secret," "mystery." They are small stones on which are written an ancient alphabetic script of Scandinavian origin that resembles hen-scratchings. When arranged in a certain order, they are used for DIVINATION purposes much like the TAROT. Typically they are arranged in three families of eight runes each, plus one blank rune. The families (Freyrs, Hagad, Tyr's) are the names of Norse gods.

SHAMAN. (Wizard, sorcerer, witchdoctor, seer.) A person who enters an altered state of consciousness to contact one or more spirits and to acquire knowledge, information or power.

SORCERY. Assumed power to manipulate and alter natural and supernatural events or states with proper knowledge of MAGIC and performance of ritual; typically understood by New Agers as being available for good or evil use. (See also WITCHCRAFT.)

SUFISM. An offshoot of Islam that emphasizes the contemplative and nuptial union with Absolute Being. The journey to such a goal will proceed through the mystical stage of concentration and apprehension of the oneness of everything, through ecstasy and union with Deity and through a sense of one's nothingness.

SYNCRETISM. The fusion of different forms of belief or practice; the claim that all religions are one and share the same core teachings.

TALISMAN. An object that is worn or carried and is believed to confer on its bearer MAGICAL powers or protection.

TAO. (Pronounced dow.) A Chinese concept of the Way, which is both a path of conduct and the principle governing the operations of the entire universe.

TAROT. A deck of picture cards used for DIVINATION or fortune-telling. Developed in its present form in the last century, it now includes twenty-two characters, among them the Magician, Death, the Pope, the Popess, the Devil, and the Fool, which represent any human on the path of life. Similar to the I CHING.

TELEKINESIS. A form of PSYCHOKINESIS or PK; the apparent movement of stationary objects without the use of any known physical force.

TELEPATHY. The silent transfer of thoughts from one mind to another; ESP of another person's mental state or thoughts.

THEISM. A Judeo-Christian belief in the one Personal Creator who is independent from, and sovereign over, His creation.

TRANCE. A HYPNOTIC-like state of consciousness, induced or spontaneous, that gives access to what are ordinarily inhibited capacities of the mind-body system. Trance states are generally self-induced.

TRANSCENDENTAL MEDITATION. TM was introduced into the United States in 1959 by Maharishi Mahesh Yogi. It is a meditative technique for achieving fulfillment, stress reduction and inner peace through contact with the transcendental

Being (reality). The movement has denied any religious connections, but it is simply a revival of ancient Hinduism.

WITCHCRAFT. A belief system supposedly handed down from ancient traditions, but is more accurately based upon the practices developed by Gerald B. Gardner (1884-1964), a British OCCULTist. These Wiccan (Old English for "male magician") groups practice ritual MAGIC and/or nature-oriented NEOPAGANISM. There are also Dianic cults that are feminist in orientation and that emphasize the traditional goddess of witchcraft. These women teach that their highest purpose in life occurs when they become incarnated with the goddess. Feminist witches believe that they have been given PSYCHIC powers.

WORLDVIEW. A common consensus about the nature of reality; a set of presuppositions or premises held consciously or unconsciously about the makeup of the cosmos.

YOGA. Literally, "yoking" or "joining"; any system or spiritual discipline by which the YOGI seeks to condition the self at all levels—physical, psychical and spiritual. The goal of this Indian religious tradition is a state of well-being, the loss of self-identity and absorption into union with the Absolute, or Ultimate Being.

YOGI. A master of one or more methods of YOGA who teaches it to others.

ZEN. A type of Buddhist thought best known for its emphasis on an experience of enlightenment, which occurs when the person is able to break away from the commitment and attachment to the logical and rational ordering of experience.

ZODIAC. The imaginary belt in the heavens that encompasses the apparent paths of the principal planets (except Pluto). It is divided into twelve constellations or signs based upon the assumed dates that the sun enters each of these "houses" or symbols. The Zodiac is used for predictions in ASTROLOGY.

Recommended Reading

New Age Rage. Karen Hoyt, (Revell, 1987)

Confronting the New Age. Douglas Groothuis, (InterVarsity Press, 1988)

Unmasking the New Age. Douglas Groothuis, (InterVarsity Press, 1986)

Revealing the New Age Jesus. Douglas Groothuis, (InterVarsity Press, 1990)

Understanding the New Age. Russell Chandler, (Word, 1988)

New Age Medicine. Reisser, Reisser, Weldon; (InterVarsity Press, 1987)

Reincarnation: A Christian Critique of a New Age Doctrine. Mark Albrecht, (InterVarsity Press, 1987)

Evangelizing the New Age. Paul McGuire, (Servant Publ., 1989)

The Universe Next Door. James Sire, (InterVarsity Press, 1988; 2nd Ed.)

Like Lambs to the Slaughter. Johanna Michaelsen, (Harvest House, 1989)

The Beautiful Side of Evil. Johanna Michaelsen, (Harvest House, 1988)

Turning Point: A Christian World View. Schlossberg and Olasky, (Crossway, 1987)

Powers: Testing the Psychic and Supernatural. Dan Korem, (InterVarsity Press, 1988)

Streetwise Parents, Foolproof Kids. Dan Korem, (NavPress, 1992)

The Secret Teachings of the Masonic Lodge: A Christian Perspective. Ankerberg and Weldon, (Moody, 1990)

A Crash Course in the New Age. Eliot Miller, (Baker, 1989)

Spiritual Disciplines for the Christian Life. Donald S. Whitney (Navpress, 1991)

Through New Eyes: Developing a Biblical View of the World. James B. Jordan, (Wolgemuth & Hyatt, 1988)

None Dare Call It Witchcraft. Gary North, (Arlington House Publ., 1976)

A Different Gospel. D.R. McConnell, (Hendrickson Publ., 1988)

Research Organizations

Christian Research Institute
P.O. Box 500
San Juan Capistrano, CA 92693-0500

Spiritual Counterfeits Project
P.O. Box 4308
Berkeley, CA 94704